Jörgen Weibull

# SWEDISH
# HISTORY
# IN OUTLINE

SVENSKA INSTITUTET

Swedish History in Outline
Second, revised edition, second printing

© 1993, 1997 Jörgen Weibull and the Swedish Institute
Translation by Paul Britten Austin
Typography by Inga Britt Liljeroth
Illustrations selected by Gil Dahlström
Maps: Tecknargården, Landskrona
Printed in Sweden by Skogs Boktryckeri AB, Trelleborg 1998
ISBN 91-520-0476-7

*Jörgen Weibull*, professor emeritus (born 1924), held professorships at the universities of Aarhus and Aalborg, Denmark (1967–77), before becoming professor of history at Gothenburg University (1977–90). He is a member of the Royal Swedish Academy of Letters, History and Antiquities and a commentator in the Swedish radio and TV on historical issues.

The author alone is responsible for the opinions expressed in this book.

———

Cover: 'Valdemar Atterdag extorting tax from Visby', oil painting by C.G. Hellquist, 1882. After recovering Skåne in the previous year, the Danish king launched a campaign against Gotland in 1361 and on July 21 bloodily defeated a local peasant army outside the Hanseatic city of Visby, where the citizens stood looking on from its walls without lifting a finger to help them. Shortly afterwards the city had to capitulate. Legend relates that Valdemar Atterdag set up three large beer barrels, which the citizens, if they did not wish to be plundered, had to fill with gold and silver. Even if not in all respects an authentic reconstruction this late nineteenth-century painting gives a good idea of the colourful and varied appearance of a mediaeval city. It is also redolent of the many wars between Sweden and Denmark, a recurrent theme in Swedish history until the early nineteenth century. Gotlands fornsal, Visby. Photo: The National Art Museums, Stockholm.

# Contents

# Prehistory

'Midvinterblot' (Sacrifice at the Winter Solstice) by Carl Larsson, 1853–1919. This Jugend-style work, measuring 13.6 x 6.4 m., depicts King Domalde being sacrificed to bring about a good harvest after years of crop failure. The scene is imagined as taking place in front of the heathen temple at Uppsala. Such objects as the carriage, the temple's mural décor, and the golden horns are taken from original finds from prehistoric and mediaeval Scandinavia, but many details are gross anachronisms. The painting, made

6

in 1914, is one of the last major national-romantic works. Carl Larsson painted it with a view to it being placed over the great staircase of the National Museum in Stockholm, but though he declared it to be 'one of the strongest and most beautiful things I've done' it was turned down. In 1987 it was sold to a Japanese buyer but is now placed in the keeping of the National Museum in Stockholm. – Photo: The National Art Museums, Stockholm.

# The Stone Age

Eleven thousand years before Christ the entire land area of what today is Sweden still lay under the ice cap, whose limit roughly coincided with the coastline of today's Skåne (Scania). South of it lay the Baltic Ice Sea.

By around 8500 BC the ice had receded to Central Sweden, whereupon the ocean, breaking through, joined the Baltic with the North Sea, thus forming the Yoldia Sea, named after a saltwater mussel characteristic of the period. But after a further 1,500 years or so the Yoldia Sea was cut off by the rising of the land mass, and its waters flowed out by the so-called Svea River through today's provinces of Västmanland and Närke into Lake Vänern, then an inlet of the Western Ocean. The Baltic – or Ancylus Lake, so-called after a freshwater shellfish – had become a freshwater lake.

Another thousand years and the ocean again broke through, this time over the tongue of land that had linked South Sweden with the continent. Again the Baltic – or Litorina Sea, as it is called when referring to this period – became saline, much more so than it is today, as it was linked with the ocean by a broad mass of water around the Danish islands. Not until about 4500 BC, however, did the Baltic and the Scandinavian land mass more or less assume their present extent and shape.

The earliest evidence of human occupation, found outside Malmö, in the south, comes from finds dating from about 8000 BC. It was then the first hunter and fisher folk moved north-

8

'Ale Stones', at Kåseberga on the south coast of Skåne, are Sweden's largest ship-burial site. Consisting of 58 stones in the shape of a 67-m. ship, the site can be dated to the Viking Age, AD 800–1050, making it one of the last funeral monuments of this kind. It is perhaps the most splendid representative of a much older tradition where the grave symbolizes the dead man's voyage to the underworld. Burial monuments with images of ships are found in Scandinavia from the early Bronze Age, c. 1800 BC. – IBL AB.

wards in the wake of the melting ice cap. A major dwelling site from about a millennium later has been discovered in a peat bog at Ageröd, by Lake Ringsjön, in Skåne; and its finds show that human subsistence in the Old Stone Age was still based on hunting and fishing. At the same time such stone artifacts as axes, arrowheads and knives, becoming steadily more refined, are evidence of population growth and cultural development.

It was during the last part of the Old Stone Age and the Litorina period that primitive methods of cultivation made their appearance. By now people were keeping domestic animals and grazing cattle. Typical of the Late Stone Age, 2500–1800 BC, are fixed settlements based on agriculture and cattle raising. A new form of burial, the so-called megalithic, with its stone chamber graves, chiefly found in the southern and western regions, indicates a cultural change that among other things has been

9

linked with the many battle or boat axes, so-called. Apparently the country had been conquered by some foreign people, who created a class society under powerful chieftains.

## The Bronze Age

During the Bronze Age, 1800–500 BC, we begin to find traces of trade contacts with the continent and the British Isles. The use of metals, mainly bronze, modifies the culture, whose class structure becomes even more marked, and there are swift developments in arts and crafts. At the same time burial customs change. Now individual graves are found under great mounds – in South Sweden in tumuli along gravel ridges, on the west coast and to the north under huge stone cairns. The wealth of bronze and gold ornaments found in these graves indicates a flourishing culture.

## The Iron Age

Iron was evidently used from the sixth century BC. Obviously the population of the southern and western regions had close contacts with the continental Celtic La Tène culture. A peasant society of fixed villages had now come into being, with both near-lying and outlying pastures. From the birth of Christ to about AD 500 Scandinavian historians speak of the Roman Iron Age, a time when trade links existed between Sweden and the Roman Empire. Rich finds of coins and ornamental objects, glass and drinking beakers show how intimate these links were. At the same time the first written information about Scandinavia is to be found: in such first-century AD Roman sources as Tacitus' *De Germania* (c. 100 AD), but also in Procopius' and Jordanes' sixth-century writings. Here we find Sweden – or more exactly Scandinavia – described as a land inhabited by a great many tribes, each under its own chieftain or king.

# The Middle Ages

## The Vendel Period

From the era known in European history as the Early Middle Ages Sweden can show many superb and idiosyncratic archeological remains. This period, from the end of the Age of Migrations in the sixth century to the beginning of the Viking Age, around AD 800, is known in Sweden as the Period of the Vendels – a name derived from the many ship burials found near Vendel Church in Uppland. Outside Uppland finds from this period are rarer, except on Gotland, where their chief characteristic is the many pictoglyphs. The Vendels' custom of burying their warriors with their helmets, swords, shields and various superb artifacts, both of indigenous and foreign manufacture, indicates a society whose wealthy and powerful chieftains traded with or travelled to foreign lands. Further emphasis on contacts with traders from both near and far comes from finds in such trading centres as Helgö, in Lake Mälaren, where we gain an impression of wealthy peasants or chieftains whose trade with countries on the other side of the Baltic presaged the great expansion of the Viking Age.

## The Viking Age

During the period between about AD 800 and 1050 the Scandinavian peoples' history bears the imprint of a violent outburst of vitality and expansion. It was this that expressed itself in Viking raids, colonization, and even in the founding of farflung Viking empires.

The earliest sure evidence of this expansion is the plundering by Danish and Norwegian Vikings in AD 793 of Lindisfarne Monastery, on Holy Island, off the English coast. Thereafter they went on to penetrate French and German rivers and, in the mid-ninth century, even got as far as Portugal and Spain, passed through the Straits of Gibraltar, and broke into the Mediterranean. In the tenth century this Danish-Norwegian expansion, in which Vikings from Skåne and the Swedish west coast participated, led to their either settling in or levying Danegeld on parts of England and Normandy. And finally, in the early eleventh century, it culminated in Canute the Great's North Sea empire. Besides Denmark and Norway he also ruled over much of England.

Pictoglyph from Hunninge at Klintehamn, Gotland. The scenes described are battles, Viking raids and assaults on the island's farms. The stone, dating from the eighth century AD, witnesses to the island's crucial role in Swedish expansion across the Baltic. – Gotlands fornsal, Visby.

13

The Swedish Viking raids emanated mainly from Uppland, the Lake Mälaren basin and Gotland, and went eastwards. Finds from those regions show that as early as the seventh and eighth centuries there had been lively communications across the Baltic. From about AD 800 onwards, Birka, on the island of Björkö in Lake Mälaren, was obviously a Baltic trading centre, whose commerce extended as far as to Byzantium and the Caliphate, in the east, and, in the west, to the kingdom of the Franks, whose written annals record in 839 that at Ingelheim an emissary from Byzantium presented himself before the Emperor Louis the Pious, together with men from *Rus*, i.e. Swedish Vikings, possibly from Roslagen, just north of present-day Stockholm. More than 1,000 items of treasure have been found – whereof 690 on Gotland. They comprise numerous Arabic coins which permit assured datings and indicate the existence of such distant trade links. But they also reveal that, around AD 1050 or shortly afterwards, this trade – or rather, this exchange of commodities – came to an abrupt end.

There is something problematic, still not properly explained, about the Scandinavian peoples' explosion of energy and expansiveness at this time. True, earlier references to the peoples of the far north had spoken of their enterprising, adventurous nature. But many other explanations can be envisaged – for instance, that climatic improvement had led to over-population. All these, however, are only theories, without any basis in observable fact. More credible, and more impressive, is the hypothesis launched by the Belgian historian Henri Pirenne. Pirenne has shown how during the seventh and eighth centuries, after Mahomet's death in AD 632, at a time when Charlemagne's empire in France and Western Germany was becoming a great power, the Islamic expansion and Arab conquest of regions along the south and east Mediterranean coasts, from the Balkans to the east to Spain in the west, had interrupted communications between Western Europe and the Orient. This meant that a war-ridden and ever more pirate-infested Mediterranean ceased to provide a communications route for or be a centre of European culture. Communications being cut between the Carolingian Empire, in the west, and, in the east, the two great powers with their capitals in Constantinople and Baghdad, traders were forced to seek out other routes, hitherto unknown.

For a long while the Viking raids, which began suddenly in the latter half of the eighth century, were regarded by historians as mere outbursts of conquest and devastation. Contemporary statements in Arabic and Russian chronicles, as well as the wealth of treasures found in Sweden and Denmark and above all

Most Swedish Viking raids went eastwards, in the eighth century to the Baltic east coast and from the mid-ninth century onwards into Russia via its rivers. The raids even reached the Black Sea and Constantinople, which the Vikings called 'Miklagård', and along the Volga to the Caspian, where they encountered merchants from the Caliphate and Baghdad. Vikings from today's southern and western Sweden also took part in the westward raids on France and England.

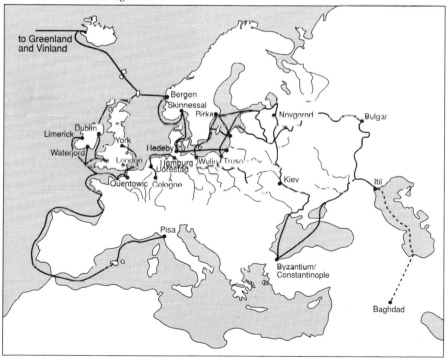

15

on Gotland, bear eloquent witness to the role played by the Viking Age in promoting trade between the Carolingian Empire and the Muslim countries around the Black and Caspian Seas.

An even knottier problem than the origins and causes of the Viking Age, however, has perhaps been how to explain why, in the second half of the eleventh century, so stupendous an outburst of vitality and expansion should have come to so abrupt an end. Here too Pirenne's theory provides a logical, not to say satisfactory explanation. The ending of the wars in the Mediterranean and suppression of piracy reopened its trade routes; and not long afterwards the Crusades gave rise to lively traffic between Western Europe and Italy, on the one hand, and Constantinople and the Near East on the other, thus removing the basis of Scandinavian prosperity and expansion.

## From Heathendom to Christianity

Before the arrival of Christianity the Scandinavian peoples had worshipped a variety of gods. Though each had a special function for society and the individual, all had their place in a colourful pantheon, headed by Odin, the war-god. At his side was Thor, the god of lightning and virility, rain and crops; but also the kindly Frej, or Frö, god of fertility. Another crucial element in this ancient Nordic religion, so well suited to the clan society existing in Sweden during the Iron and Viking Ages, was ancestor worship. The ancient gods, who have figured extensively in Swedish and Scandinavian art and literature – and indeed still do – live on in many a Swedish place name.

It was during the Viking Age that the Swedes first came into contact with Christianity. The first Christian missionary to set foot in the country was Ansgar, a monk sent out by the Emperor Louis the Pious. In the years 830–831, and again in 850, Ansgar visited Birka, before ending his days as archbishop of Hamburg-Bremen. But his church at Birka proved transient. More than a century had to pass before, at the end of the 900s, we hear of

16

English missionaries in the province of Västergötland, which was then converting to the new faith. Not until the end of the eleventh century, on the other hand, did Christianity really strike root in the Mälaren basin, where the Uppsala temple had been one of the old religion's chief cult centres; and only in the 1120s do we hear of a firmly organized Swedish church, with bishop-rics at Skara, Linköping, Eskilstuna, Västerås and Sigtuna.

Christianity's triumph was a cultural revolution in itself, but also instrumental in replacing tribal society by an organized state. In 1164 the first archbishop of Sweden was installed at Uppsala. And the papal bull establishing his archbishopric is also our oldest source to give contemporary evidence that Sweden was by now an autonomous realm, under a single king.

## Uniting and Organizing the Realm

The nature of the process by which Sweden became a kingdom, however, has long been a matter of dispute. The main point at issue used to be the point in time at which it was united. One school of thought, based on the English Beowulf Saga and archeological evidence, maintained that the first king to rule the whole country could be dated to prior to AD 800, possibly even as early as the sixth century. Other historians only found sure evidence from the mid-eleventh. Both theories, however, as-sumed that the realm came into being as a result of the Svear, living in the central parts of present-day Sweden, conquering Götaland, to the south, and that the realm therefore centred on Lake Mälaren, more precisely in Uppland, with Uppsala as its chief place.

Later research takes a different view. It now seems that Sweden's cradle lay in Götaland, where the ever-warring royal clans demonstrably stemmed from and had long had their domains. It is this view which sees in the country's conversion to Christianity an important condition for its transformation from a tribal community to a single united kingdom. Certainly the

17

conversions of the provinces of Västergötland and Östergötland long antedated that of the Mälaren region, and it was also there, as early as the first half of the twelfth century, the first monasteries were founded.

But how important, in reality, was the country's formal union? Our eleventh and twelfth-century sources are unambiguous. It was the province, headed by its magistrate *(jarl)*, or perhaps by some local king, that was responsible for justice and administration. Not until the second half of the thirteenth century can we speak of any significant central administration comprising the whole country.

The first person who can be said with any certainty to have been king of all Sweden is Olof Skötkonung. Just before the year 1000 he had been baptized at Skara, in Västergötland; and coins struck in the following decades at Sigtuna, in Uppland, witness to his rule over Svealand. Whether he in fact ruled the whole country, however, is impossible to determine, and it is certain that under his successors the realm again split up. Again and again we hear of more than one king ruling simultaneously in its various regions.

Not until the 1130s does Sweden, under Sverker the Elder, seem to have definitively become one kingdom. In the 1150s another clan, led by Erik Jedvardsson, later to be known as Saint Erik, gained power over the whole realm, and for a century thereafter a struggle for power between the two clans would place now the Sverkers, now the Eriks on the throne. By this time, however, the realm had obviously been united, as can be seen from the 1164 papal bull instituting the Uppsala archbishopric. Even so, it may still be reasonably asked whether, in point of power and authority, the individual provinces were not in reality still independent entities. Their extant law codes, written down in the thirteenth century, seem to point in that direction.

18

In almost all respects the thirteenth century was a time of swift expansion and development. Great areas of new land came under the plough, and others yielded bigger crops. Trade was organized, towns were founded. The church was definitively integrated in the international organization, and canon law generally accepted. At the same time the social structure was radically modified by the rise of a secular nobility. And it is now the king's central authority assumes a firm and definite shape.

Agriculture, supplemented by hunting and fishing, was basic to the economy. Though populated and cultivated since Viking times, the villages of the great central plains – Västergötland, Östergötland, Närke and the Mälaren region – were assuming a more definite organization. Arable land was partitioned in such a way that each farm had its share of every field. All work was organized by the village council, and grain output rose. At the same time the forest lands of Småland, Värmland and Dalarna were being colonized. Mainly they would produce cattle and a surplus of such products as meat and butter.

These surpluses and an ever more differentiated agricultural output stimulated trade. At the same time international commerce was growing. The Hanseatic League, its Baltic trade mainly managed from Lübeck, came into being. Exports of such Swedish products as meat and butter, furs, herring and other fish grew, and on the coastal estuaries they gave rise to new towns whose populations of craftsmen and merchants – at first mainly of German origin – now began to constitute a new social group: the town burghers.

The thirteenth century is also the great era of Swedish church-building. By now the country was divided up into parishes, each of which built itself a church, often of stone, many of which still stand and witness to this, the first great age of Catholicism in Sweden. In 1248 a convention held at Skänninge in Östergötland introduced celibacy for the clergy and established the church's right to collect tithes. Now canon law, applicable to all

19

clerics and in the parishes, begins to influence secular juridic ideas, for instance of land ownership. No longer is land the outright property of family or clan; it may also be bequeathed to the church and its institutions. Lastly, the church's servants and estates were exempted from secular taxation. A spiritual aristocracy came into being.

Both king and magnates had at an early stage surrounded themselves with retainers and men-at-arms. Magnates and the wealthier peasantry alike undertook, in lieu of various taxes and other obligations, military and hospitable, to serve the Crown in war. In this way the late thirteenth century also saw the establishment of a secular aristocracy; at the same time laws, binding on the whole realm, were promulgated, guaranteeing individual immunity.

During the century's later decades the kingdom became organized in fiefs *(län)* or counties, each taxed and centrally administered from some permanent fortress or castle. Simultaneously the central power, headed by the king, assumed firmer shape. A Council came into being, with a Lord Chief Justice *(drots)*, an Earl Marshal *(marsk)* and a Chancellor *(kansler)*, responsible respectively for law, the army and the administration.

Though Valdemar, nephew of the last king of the Erik clan, was elected at the latter's death in 1250, power passed effectively into the hands of Birger Jarl, the boy's guardian and father. After defeating all his rivals he had the Crown confirmed as resident in the so-called Folkunga dynasty.

Whereas the country's political history during the 1150–1250 period had been one of bitter strife between the Eriks and the Sverkers, the Folkunga period (1250–1364) was to be marked by internal struggles within this new dynasty, beginning with a revolt, supported by Denmark and certain disaffected magnates, by Valdemar's two brothers Magnus and Erik. In 1275, Valdemar was defeated at the battle of Hova; and Magnus, nicknamed Ladulås (literally *the Barn Lock*), was elected king and reigned until his death in 1290. It was his reign that saw the

Legend has it that Saint Erik made a 'crusade' into Finland to baptize its population. Here depicted in a fifteenth-century copper relief on the sarcophagus of Finland's patron saint Bishop Henrik in Nousis church, Finland. The legend sprung up in the mid-thirteenth century, when the Swedish conquest of Finland was undertaken by Birger Jarl's government and completed by Torgils Knutsson. It was also in the thirteenth century that the south-west region of Finland began to be colonized in earnest by Swedes. The earliest extant documents witnessing to this conquest are from 1303, and in 1323 the frontier between Sweden and the Russian grand duchy of Novgorod was fixed by the Treaty of Nöteborg. To the south it ran along the Syster, in the Karelian promontory. – Bra Böcker Archives.

establishment of a regular nobility, by the Alsnö Decree of 1280. In the following year, probably as a concession to the very groups which had brought Magnus into power, ecclesiastical privileges, too, were confirmed.

Since Magnus' eldest son Birger was still a minor at his father's death in 1290, power was taken over by the Council

21

under the Earl Marshal, Torgils Knutsson. Under Knutsson's energetic leadership large parts of Finland were conquered, its frontier with Russia was established on the Neva, and the town of Viborg was founded. At the same time his anti-clerical policy led to conflicts with the young king and his two brothers, Dukes Erik and Valdemar. In 1306 Torgils Knutsson was deposed, and a struggle broke out between Birger and his two brothers, power passing to and fro until, in 1317, Birger invited them to a banquet at Nyköping and had them assassinated. This led to a revolt and his deposition. In his place Duke Erik's three-year-old son Magnus Eriksson was elected king in 1319.

It was at his election that a Letter of Privilege was promulgated that has been called Sweden's Magna Carta and also its first constitution. In it the great men of the realm, both secular and ecclesiastical, swore absolute fealty to the boy king they had just elected, while the king undertook

- not to impose new taxes without the consent of the Council
- not to appoint any foreigner councillor or castle bailiff, and finally
- to govern by law, and not imprison anyone, whether rich or poor, without due examination and judgment in process of law.

Each of these clauses would later be incorporated unchanged into the code of laws, valid for the whole kingdom, promulgated by Magnus Eriksson around 1350, and again in Kristoffer's code, ratified in 1442.

The fourteenth century saw a swift development in communications, both economic and cultural, with the countries of western Europe. Swedish towns and their trade were dominated by Lübeck and the Hanseatic League, a German influence that reached its climax during the reign of Albrekt of Mecklenburg (1364–89). The versified Erik Chronicle, dating from the 1320s or 1330s and depicting the history of the Folkunga dynasty, bears witness to the arrival in Sweden of courtly poetry and

22

Saint Birgitta (Bridget) – sculpture in wood from Östra Ryd, Uppland, now in the Museum of National Antiquities, Stockholm. Herself a scion of a wealthy family, Birgitta married a lawman, Ulf Gudmarsson, with whom she had eight children. After his death in 1344 she settled at Alvastra Monastery, Östergötland, and founded another at Vadstena, on Lake Vättern, to which King Magnus Eriksson in 1346 donated an estate. In 1349 she left Sweden and thereafter mainly lived in Rome, up to her death in 1373. – ATA, Stockholm.

continental-style notions of chivalry. Through her writings and her foundation, the Bridgettine Order, Saint Birgitta (Bridget) (1303–73), herself a member of the reigning house and a woman of education and culture, became eminent in European affairs.

His election had made Magnus Eriksson king both over Sweden and Norway, whose Crown he, in the same year, had just inherited from Håkon Magnusson, his maternal grandfather. On coming of age in 1332 he also acquired by purchase the southernmost provinces of Skåne and Blekinge. Halland he had already inherited from his mother, Duchess Ingeborg.

Magnus Eriksson's reign would be marked by his conflicts with the magnates, who objected to his efforts to assert himself, e.g. by appointing his son Erik joint regent and heir to the throne during his own lifetime. The Council also accused him of relying on foreign advisers. On the other hand the great nobles also forced him to introduce the constitutional stipulations of the 1319 Letter of Privilege into the law of the land and thus accept them for the future.

In the 1350s opposition to his régime burst out into open rebellion, and in 1364 he was driven into exile – not, however, before the Danes under Valdemar Atterdag in 1360 had reconquered Skåne, Halland and Blekinge and, in 1361, even seized Gotland and Visby, that island's important trading city. Nor did Albrekt of Mecklenburg's election to the Swedish throne in 1364 end the power struggle between Crown and nobles, who in the end called in Valdemar Atterdag's daughter and successor, Queen Margareta of Denmark (widow of Magnus Eriksson's son Håkan) in order to jointly elect her and her son Olof, still a minor, to the throne. Upon Olof dying in 1387, Queen Margareta herself was recognized in 1388 as Sweden's 'plenipotentiary Mistress and true Lord'. Since she had already been recognized as ruler of Denmark and Norway, this meant that she, in her own person, united the three Scandinavian countries in a single union.

## The Kalmar Union, 1389–1521

Behind the later fourteenth century's proliferation of conflicts between Crown and nobility had lain the late mediaeval agrarian crisis. As elsewhere, it caused the population to dwindle, farmsteads to be abandoned and agricultural output to fall. Affecting as it did the whole of western Europe, the crisis' causes and consequences are perhaps the problem most discussed by mediaevalists, both in Scandinavia and abroad.

In Sweden it was precipitated by the Black Death. Striking the country in 1349–50, we see from the sources how the plague wiped out whole villages and raised mortality to hitherto unknown levels. Worst ravaged seem to have been the forest and border regions, i.e. those most recently cultivated. The older plainlands seem to have been rather less grievously afflicted, though even there the devastation varied widely from one region to another. The upshot was a drop in population, huge numbers of deserted farms, reduced output and higher living costs. Not until the mid-fifteenth century can any improvement be discerned. Only then would the abandoned farms be reoccupied, and the worst afflicted areas again be cultivated. Simultaneously the country's agricultural output changes character. Cattle breeding increases at the expense of grain output, and this in turn leads to greater exports of such products as meat and butter.

The union of the three Scandinavian countries under a single ruler, ratified at an assembly at Kalmar in 1397, also changed the political scene. Margareta's nephew, Erik of Pomerania, was then recognized as king of all three countries, and the Crown, represented by Margareta herself, formally undertook not to interfere with each people's laws and privileges. All important positions were to be filled with native Swedes, Danes or Norwegians respectively.

The reign of Margareta until her death in 1412 augmented the power of the Crown; economically by reducing noble estates and politically – her promise not to appoint foreigners being forgotten – by appointing her confidants to all important posts. Although this aggravated the tension between Crown and nobility, matters would not reach breaking point until in the reign of Erik of Pomerania (1412–39). But then it led to open revolt.

Margareta's conflict with Albrekt of Mecklenburg and his supporters had obliged her to come to terms with the Hanseatic League, whose economic domination in Scandinavia had been confirmed. Erik of Pomerania, by contrast, tried to free himself from economic and political dependence on Lübeck and the League. This led to a war which not merely imposed heavier dues and taxes on the Swedish population, but also interrupted the country's chief commercial links, adversely affecting, among much else, its crucial iron exports, and thus crippling the Bergslagen mining and iron-making district. This in turn explains why the great revolt against Erik, led by Engelbrekt Engelbrektsson, a member of a wealthy mining family, should have started in Dalarna.

After initial successes had gained it the nobles' and Council's

Stockholm at the time of the coronation of Kristian II, in 1520. Below, a series of pictures of the Stockholm Bloodbath – coloured copper engraving from 1676, based on a woodcut made in 1524 by two Antwerp artists at Gustav Vasa's instigation. Left: Kristian II, flanked by bishops, is about to enter the city. Storkyrkan, the main church where he was crowned, is exaggerated. In front of it can be seen the royal 'Three Crowns' castle and behind it the Franciscan friary on Riddarholmen, then known as Greyfriars

Island. The lower series shows Kristian II receiving guests at the coronation banquet; then the king and Gustav Trolle indicting them; Bishop Vincent and others being beheaded for heresy; their heads being flung into barrels as their bodies are dragged away to be burnt. Lastly, Kristian II's sanguinary visitation of the realm. An item of early Gustav Vasa propaganda, the woodcut is nevertheless valuable for its detailed depiction of mediaeval Stockholm. – Det Kongelige Bibliotek, Copenhagen.

support, Engelbrekt, having been elected Captain-General *(rikshövitsman)*, was shortly afterwards murdered. But the struggle went on, this time under Karl Knutsson Bonde, the nobles' leader. But though his election as Protector of the Realm in 1438 effectively put paid to Erik's power in Sweden and led to his deposition, the winner in the ensuing struggle for the Crown was Erik's nephew, Kristoffer of Bavaria. This meant that the Union was formally retained; Kristoffer, however, was obliged to concede so much to the nobles' demands that it was they who, in Sweden, de facto retained all power.

The later half of the fifteenth century saw Sweden divided up into a number of non-hereditary fiefs, ruled from castles, whence it was in all essentials administered while the incumbents struggled for power over the realm as a whole. At the same time there was a struggle for power between the nobility and the Union kings. After his victory at Brunkeberg in 1471 power passed to Sten Sture the Elder, who, with brief interruptions, would rule as Protector until his death in 1503. In the ensuing internecine struggles Kristian II of Denmark intervened. In 1517, with the aid of his supporters within the Swedish nobility, he tried to restore the Union by force of arms. After two unsuccessful attempts to take Stockholm (in 1517 and 1518) he finally won a battle on the ice on Lake Åsunden, where his chief opponent, Sten Sture the Younger, was mortally wounded. Stockholm capitulated shortly afterwards, and Kristian II had himself proclaimed king, after which all his leading opponents, accused of heresy, were beheaded in the great market place. Whether this massacre, the so-called Stockholm Bloodbath, was instigated by Kristian himself or was just the final catastrophe in the power struggle between the various Swedish parties, is another much discussed topic.

# The Vasa dynasty and Sweden's Period as a Great Power, 1521–1718

# The Reformation and the Founding of the National State

A member of a noble family which had opposed Kristian II and who himself had escaped the Bloodbath was Gustav Vasa. Taken hostage by Kristian II in 1518, he had been imprisoned in Denmark, escaped to Lübeck, and thence returned to Sweden. Hearing of the terrible events in Stockholm, he went north to Dalarna, hoping to muster support for a revolt. The Dalesmen had suffered severely under the Danish bailiffs' oppression and from the interruption of the Lübeck trade, and after some initial hesitation they decided to support him. Meanwhile another revolt had broken out in the forests of Småland. The rebels' swift successes gained them the support of most of the nobility, and in August 1521 Gustav Vasa was elected Protector.

However, Kristian II still held Stockholm as well as certain castles, and also had command of the seas. So Gustav Vasa turned to Lübeck and with its help recovered the Danish-occupied castles. At an assembly at Strängnäs on June 6, 1523,

State regalia for Erik XIV's magnificent coronation in 1561. They symbolize the power of the Crown, strongly asserted by Swedish kings in the sixteenth and seventeenth centuries. The crown is the traditional symbol of royalty. The sceptre signifies the temporal power; the orb, engraved with a map of the world, empire. The key of state, unique to Sweden and introduced on that occasion, symbolizes the monarch's power to lock out evil and protect the good. All these regalia were made by Dutch goldsmiths in Stockholm. – The Royal Treasury, Stockholm.

Gustav Vasa in the 1550s. Contemporary portrait by Willem Boy. Thanks to his numerous letters Gustav Vasa's personality is better known to us than that of any other sixteenth-century Swede. They are on every conceivable topic, large or small. The king expresses himself, often drastically, with personal force and eloquence. Himself originally a landowner, he ran the realm as if it were one big farm. – The National Art Museums, Stockholm.

he was elected King of Sweden, and shortly thereafter, on Midsummer Day 1523, entered Stockholm. The entire country had been liberated.

But Lübeck's support had been costly. To liquidate this debt Gustav Vasa had to burden his subjects with extra taxes. This not sufficing, and since the ecclesiastical estates comprised 21 per cent of all homesteads (as against only 5.5 per cent in the Crown's possession) he turned to the church, asking for a special contribution of silver and tithes. The request was refused.

Meanwhile Martin Luther's doctrines had begun to penetrate the country. Olaus Petri's Swedish translation of the New Testament had appeared in 1526, and in Stockholm the Mass was beginning to be celebrated in the vernacular. In these financial straits Gustav, in June 1527, summoned a parliament.

Olaus Magnus was a Swedish priest whom Gustav Vasa sent to Rome in 1523. When the Reformation came he remained abroad, and in 1544 the Pope made him archbishop of Sweden. His magnum opus *Historia de gentibus septentrionalibus* (The History of the Nordic Peoples), published in 1555, describes the geographical conditions, fauna, popular customs, economy and industry of Scandinavia. The pictures above show the harvest being brought in; and corn and other grain being made into beer. – The Royal Library, Stockholm.

Meeting at Västerås, it sanctioned a decree known as the Västerås Recess, under which the church was to surrender part of its income to the Crown, likewise all its castles and all donations made later than 1454. The decision broke the power of the bishops and stripped the church of virtually all its estates, most of which went to the Crown. Doctrine was reformed along Lutheran lines and a state church was set up, where the word of God was to be 'preached in all its purity'. All these decisions were ultimately ratified at a convention in Uppsala in 1593.

The Västerås Recess and its implementation, however, unleashed several revolts, all crushed with a heavy hand by Gustav Vasa, who simultaneously introduced reforms to reinforce the central power of the state. A German-type exchequer was set up to collect taxes and manage the realm's finances. Likewise a chancery assisted the king, notably in foreign affairs, managed his correspondence and drew up his decrees. By concentrating all power in the king's hands via a centralized administration these reforms turned Sweden into a powerful and unified monarchy. In 1544, at a second meeting at Västerås, the elective system was abolished, and the Crown was declared hereditary in the Vasa family.

## Economy and Social Classes

Early sixteenth-century Sweden was still totally dominated by agriculture and cattle grazing; and gradually, as the century went on, the recession caused by the late mediaeval agrarian crisis gave way to a steady expansion, both of output and population. On the one hand this led to regions hitherto either uninhabited or only thinly populated being colonized; on the other, in those more densely populated, to homesteads being parcelled up. There the farms were clustered in villages, and the land, held in common, was also communally cultivated – all in contrast to the often widely isolated farms in the thinly populated and forest areas.

There was one great difference between Sweden and virtually all other European countries. A very high proportion of her peasants were self-owning. In Sweden itself more than 45 per cent of all farms, and no less than 62 per cent in Sweden-Finland, were owned by the families who cultivated them. Gustav Vasa's seizure of church lands had raised the Crown's holdings to some 30 per cent of the total, whilst the noble estates, exempt from Crown taxes, amounted to hardly 25 per cent in Sweden and, in Sweden-Finland to only 17 per cent.

This social structure and property distribution, however, was now to be modified. In the reign of Gustav II Adolf (1611–32) Sweden became involved in the continental wars – first in the Baltic provinces and Poland, then in the Thirty Years War in Germany. To finance these great wars and recompense the aristocracy, and more especially the nobility, for its contributions to the war effort, the Crown was obliged to alienate, not merely many of its own estates, but also tax-yielding homesteads. Great donations of land were made, and purchases of other land were also permitted. Though this, in the short term, enabled the Crown to finance the country's war effort, in the long run such donations reduced its annual income to a point where the whole economy ran into insoluble problems.

By the mid-seventeenth century, as a result of such gifts, the aristocracy and nobility were in receipt of taxes and dues from over 60 per cent of all homesteads. And a repossession of noble estates had become imperative. In the reign of Karl XI (1672–97), this led, in the 1680s, to the Great Reduction – a radical redistribution of landownership which brought the Crown's possessions up to 36 per cent of the whole, reduced the nobility's and aristocracy's to 33 per cent, and left 31 per cent, all of it subject to tax, to self-owning peasants. Parallel with this development and thanks not least to peasant support the reigns of Karl XI and Karl XII (1680–1718) saw the introduction and establishment of an absolute monarchy.

All through the sixteenth century Swedish towns had still been very small and populated largely by craftsmen. Only a few

34

where overseas trade was important – e.g. Stockholm, Kalmar and Söderköping – could boast influential groups of wealthy merchants, many of German origin.

Upon Frederik I of Denmark dying in 1534, war broke out between Denmark and Lübeck, the Hanseatic city having refused to recognize Frederik's son Prince Kristian as King of Denmark. In this struggle – the so-called Count's Feud – Gustav Vasa sided with Kristian. Lübeck was defeated, and in the peace that followed in 1536 the city lost not only its profitable privileges but also the great credits remaining to it in Sweden ever since the war of liberation. Sweden, no longer so heavily indebted, was now free to conduct her own trade and foreign policies. From now on she began to turn instead to the new commercial powers in the west, and during the seventeenth century this among other things forged close links with the newly liberated Netherlands, notably Amsterdam.

From the beginning of the new century trade was favoured as an element in Karl IX's and Gustav II Adolf's foreign policy. Many new towns were founded, mainly on the coastal estuaries. At the same time all towns were divided up into two categories: staple towns and hinterland towns, only the former being allowed to engage in foreign trade. Not that Sweden's great trading efforts, even transoceanic ones, amounted to much. Such Swedish colonies as New Sweden, in Delaware, and Cabo Corso, on the Gold Coast, did not survive very long, nor did they yield the expected profits.

The seventeenth century also saw a massive rise in output, strongly supported by the Crown, from the ironworks in Central Sweden. They imported Walloon smiths from the Low Countries, and other able craftsmen, mainly Germans, who helped to establish the metallurgical industry which would afterwards be so crucial to the country's economy.

In the Middle Ages it had been the ecclesiastical aristocracy which had been regarded as constituting the realm's First Estate. But after their castles, with the 1527 Västerås Parliament's approval, had been seized by the Crown, its status had become

35

Louis De Geer. A Dutch financier, in the first half of the seventeenth century he helped Sweden to obtain loans needed to finance her wars. In about 1620 he moved to Sweden and took over the management of the Crown's arms factories. In this he was so successful that during the Thirty Years War Sweden was able not merely to equip her own armies, but even exported considerable quantities of weapons. De Geer brought in immigrant labour to employ on his many estates. Most were Walloons, who greatly helped to develop the Swedish ironworks. He has been called the father of Swedish industry. – Contemporary painting by David Beck, Leufsta. Pressens Bild.

more modest. Bishops were no longer recruited from among the country's most eminent families, and by this time most of the Lutheran clergy – unlike their forerunners, who had been noblemen – were either of peasant stock or else, clerical celibacy having been done away with, came from clerical families.

Numerically the sixteenth-century Swedish nobility was a very small class. Even as late as 1600 all its male adults only amounted to 440 persons. Almost all, however, owned estates, and since as the century went on they became more and more involved in the administration, they were soon well on the way to becoming a class of well-to-do officials. At the same time the distinction between 'high' and 'low' aristocracy – nobles, one might say, and aristocrats – was becoming steadily more marked, until in the end the gulf between the tiny but wealthy and influential class of nobles, on the one hand, and the rural aristocracy, who stood close to the peasantry, on the other, grew so wide and deep that in 1626 the distinction between 'high' and 'low' aristocracy was formally regularized in the statutes of the House of Nobility, whose members were separated into two distinct classes. During the seventeenth century there was a sharp rise in the House's membership, mainly due to the many new ennoblements in connection with the great wars; but also to the great number of new posts in the various central administrative bodies set up under the 1634 Constitution and in local administrations under the Crown's provincial governors, all such posts being occupied by landless aristocrats, who had swiftly come to outnumber the landowning nobles. And it was this development which reached its climax in the 1680s, in

Swedes negotiating with American Indians, an illustration in Campanius Holm's 'Brief Account of the Province of New Sweden in America', 1702. After the Dutch had conquered the little Swedish colony on the Delaware in 1655, they offered to let the Swedes retain part of it if they would join with them in attacking the Indians. But the Swedish governor Risingh rejected the proposal as 'despicable', saying he did not want to 'entangle himself in hatred and warfare with the savages' – evidence of the Swedes' unusually good relations with the indigenous population. – The Royal Library, Stockholm.

connection with the Great Reduction. Around the turn of the new century only one aristocrat in three was a landowner, and the nobility itself had become a corps of Crown officials.

## Crown *vs.* Aristocracy

Throughout the 1521–1718 period domestic politics were dominated by a power struggle between king and aristocracy. By eliminating virtually all the leaders of the nobility the Stockholm Bloodbath had opened the way for a strong monarchy, and Gustav Vasa, seizing his opportunity, had energetically suppressed all attempts at opposition. Not until the reign of his immediate successor, Erik XIV (1560–68), had the nobility, supported by Erik's younger brothers Dukes Johan and Karl, again claimed its share of power. Though Johan and Karl, under Gustav Vasa's will, had both received dukedoms where they exerted great influence over the administration, Erik XIV forced through a modification of this arrangement, himself retaining direct control of all administration and justice, even in the duchies. This had precipitated a fierce struggle – primarily between Erik and Johan – in which the nobility had sided with the latter – a schism still further aggravated by Erik XIV's imposition of new and more onerous rules for the nobility's wartime service to the Crown. Himself almost pathologically suspicious by nature, Erik XIV indicted its leaders of high treason, executed several, and finally murdered several others with his own hand. In 1568 the nobility rebelled, deposed Erik, and imprisoned him for life.

Initially the reign of his brother Johan III (1568–92) saw a strengthening of the nobility's position. In 1569 it was granted new privileges and at the same time an attempt was made to limit the royal powers by binding the king to rule only in collaboration with the nobility and with the consent of the Council – a demand Johan III refused to accede to, and whose only effect was to increase tension with the nobility.

Not until Johan III's death in 1592, however, and after Duke Karl had seized power, did the conflict come to a head. Now the nobility supported Johan III's son and successor Sigismund, who had simultaneously become King of Poland. Defeating Sigis-

Georg von Rosen's latter-day historical portrait of Erik XIV (1871) did much to fix the popular image of that unfortunate monarch. He is seen seated between his mistress, later his wife, Karin Månsdotter and his adviser and secretary, the ill-fated Göran Persson. The document on his knee is the Stures' death sentence, which Göran Persson is trying to get him to sign, while a terrified Karin Månsdotter is trying to dissuade him. Strongly romanticized, the painting is meant as an allegory of the struggle between good and evil in the king's nature. – The National Art Museums, Stockholm.

During the first half of the seventeenth century Axel Oxenstierna was the country's leading statesman. Appointed to the Council of State in 1609, he became Chancellor in 1612. But on the death of Karl IX in the previous year he had already become the leader of the nobility, and it was he who forced through the oath to rule with their consent which Gustavus Adolphus was obliged to sign. During the latter's reign Oxenstierna did much to reform the administration and after the king's death in battle in 1632 he became the unquestioned arbiter of Swedish policies, both in what concerned the 1634 Constitution and the successful military and foreign policies during the last phase of the Thirty Years War. – The Royal Library, Stockholm.

mund, Karl, who in 1599 seized power as Protector, had the leading nobles executed (the Linköping Bloodbath in 1600) and in 1604 was crowned Karl IX. It was during his reign, 1599–1611, that the absolute monarchy which had been the work of Gustav Vasa and which, if only briefly, had also been exerted by Erik XIV, was reintroduced.

Upon Karl IX's sudden demise in 1611 his eldest son and heir, Gustav Adolf, was only 17. This, under the 1604 Order of Succession, made him a minor, and the government was to be taken over by a regency. Just then, however, Sweden was at war with Denmark and the situation was critical. Parliament, together with the nobility and its leader, Axel Oxenstierna, therefore proposed that Gustav Adolf should succeed forthwith, at the same time drawing up rules which in all essentials implied the immediate implementation of all the nobility's long-standing demands. In his oath the young king undertook not to make laws, declare war or peace or form alliances without the Estates' and Council's consent, nor to impose any new taxes without first consulting the Council. Lastly, all high administrative positions were to be reserved for Swedish noblemen.

Though Gustav II Adolf was a very strong personality, his close collaboration with his chancellor Axel Oxenstierna reduced the tension between Crown and nobility, notwithstanding his having set aside such undertakings in his oath as limited his own authority. At the same time a firm administration was organized during his reign and this increased aristocratic influence, an arrangement which would be ratified after his death at the Battle of Lützen in 1632. Indeed the 1634 Constitution placed all administrative authority in the hands of five high state officials, each with his own department.

This arrangement, imposed by the leading nobles in the Council, was however unacceptable both to Queen Kristina, after she had come of age in 1644, and to her successor Karl X Gustav (1654–60). Nor would its division of powers again be enforced until during the regency set up after the latter's death. And it would be under this regency (1660–72) that the despotic rule of the nobility, under its chancellor Magnus Gabriel De la Gardie, reached its apogée.

The tendency toward serfdom had never been so pronounced in Sweden as in other European countries. But now the nobility's extensive powers over both administration and justice on its enormous estates had come to constitute a threat to peasant liberties. And at the same time the landless and ever-growing 'low' aristocracy turned against the nobility. An acute economic crisis, due to the 1675–79 war with Denmark (the so-called Skåne War), gave rise to parliamentary demands from the three lower Estates for an enquiry into the regency's proceedings and for a Reduction. The investigation, together with the Crown's peremptory resumption of many such estates, definitively terminated the nobility's power. These radical measures and parliamentary support gave instead all power to the king. As for the once so mighty Council, after first being reduced to a merely advisory capacity, it was finally done away with altogether.

Thus ended almost two centuries of struggle. They would be followed by the Carolinian autocracy. It would last from 1680 to 1718.

41

Gustav Vasa's support for Kristian III in the war between Denmark and Lübeck in 1534–36 had led to peace between Sweden and Denmark. Under the 1524 settlement, after Kristian II had been deposed in both countries, Denmark had controlled and levied tolls on all trade passing through the Öresund Strait and the Belts, and had retained Gotland. This meant that throughout the sixteenth century she had dominated the Baltic. Her domination, however, was challenged by Erik XIV, and for almost 250 years the main goal of Swedish foreign policy would be to gain control of the area. As a first step in this direction Estonia was acquired in 1561. This gave Sweden control of a large part of the Russian trade. The goal of Swedish policy being to get into the Russian market while at the same time extending Swedish links with western Europe, this led to war with Denmark. But the so-called Nordic Seven Years War (1563–70) had ended with defeat; and under the Peace of Stettin Sweden even had to pay a heavy ransom to regain the fortress of Älvsborg, her only direct outlet to the North Sea, captured by the Danes and key to the Göta River.

In 1611 commercial rivalries, particularly the Danish Öresund tolls and the two countries' struggle for the Russian market, unleashed another conflict. Being chiefly a struggle over the Kalmar and Älvsborg fortresses, it is known as the Kalmar War. The Danes capturing both fortresses, under the Peace of Knäred (1613) they again had to be ransomed. This, however, would be the last time Denmark would successfully defend her domination of the Baltic.

In 1618 the Thirty Years War broke out; and in 1625, Scandinavia being threatened by the Catholic armies, Kristian IV had vainly tried to intervene in it. Next year he was crushingly defeated at Lutter am Barenberge. The whole of Jylland (Jutland) and some parts of the Baltic coast were occupied by the imperial armies, and Denmark was forced out of the war. Now it was Sweden's turn to be threatened.

42

Queen Kristina as a child. She was six when her father, Gustavus Adolphus, died in 1632. Declared of age in 1644 she took over the government and three years later showed strength of will by refusing to marry her cousin Karl Gustav, whom she instead, by adroit political manoeuvring, got elected as her successor. In 1654 she abdicated in his favour, left the country, converted to Catholicism and settled down in Rome. Her tomb is in St Peter's. – The Swedish Portrait Archives, Gripsholm.

In 1617 Gustav II Adolf had successfully concluded the long war against Russia with the Peace of Stolbova. In the 1620s, turning against Poland, he conquered Livonia (Latvia), and in 1629, by the armistice at Altmark, forced the Poles to surrender the right to levy tolls in certain important Baltic harbours.

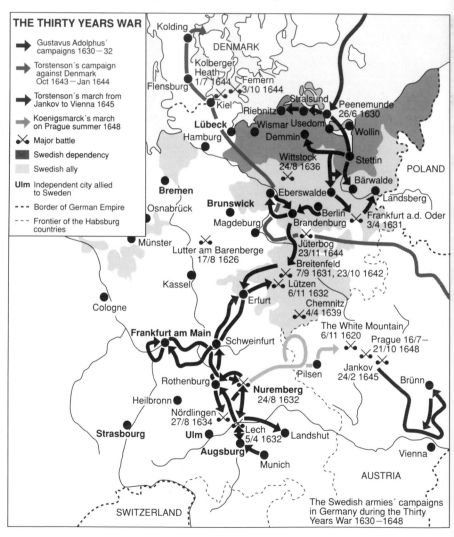

THE THIRTY YEARS WAR

Gustavus Adolphus' campaigns 1630—32

Torstenson's campaign against Denmark Oct 1643—Jan 1644

Torstenson's march from Jankov to Vienna 1645

Koenigsmarck's march on Prague summer 1648

✗ Major battle

Swedish dependency

Swedish ally

**Ulm** Independent city allied to Sweden

- - - Border of German Empire

- - - Frontier of the Habsburg countries

The Swedish armies' campaigns in Germany during the Thirty Years War 1630–1648

Finally, in 1630, Gustav Adolf intervened against the Catholic League. Winning a brilliant victory at Breitenfeld in 1631, he set up his headquarters at Mainz, where the German Protestant princes and the ambassadors of France, Holland and Britain sued him for his support. After taking Nuremberg, Augsburg and Munich in the spring and vigorously supporting the Protestant princes, his army, on November 6, 1632, confronted the imperials at Lützen. But though he defeated them, the 'Lion of the North' himself was killed in action.

Determined to persevere with his policies, his great chancellor, Axel Oxenstierna, in 1633 succeeded in bringing together the Protestant princes in the so-called Heilbronn League – which, however, would be dissolved in the following year after a crushing Swedish defeat at Nördlingen. Though the war was pursued with varying success, fortune would not again favour the Swedish arms until 1636, when France intervened actively on their side. In 1638–41 the Swedish army, commanded by Johan Banér, campaigned successfully along the Elbe and conquered large parts of southern Germany – successes which were followed up by Lennart Torstenson in his 1641–43 campaigns. Since Denmark had been becoming steadily more hostile since 1636 the Council decided that, without any declaration of war, the Swedish army under Lennart Torstenson should attack Jutland from the south.

In 1644, Swedish troops occupied Jutland, and advanced victoriously into the two mainland Danish provinces of Skåne and Blekinge. Under the Peace of Brömsebro (1645) Sweden obtained, Jämtland, Härjedalen, Gotland, Ösel and, for a period of thirty years, Halland. Furthermore, Sweden's exemption from tolls and customs dues in the Öresund was extended to Finland and her Baltic provinces, which had previously had to pay them. This meant that Denmark had lost control of the Baltic.

In 1648, after resuming its campaigns in southern Germany, the Swedish army entered Prague. It was these Swedish successes which set their stamp on the Peace of Westphalia. Under it

45

'A Splendid and Blissful Occasion', the festive procession through Stockholm in October, 1650, on the occasion of Queen Kristina's coronation. She did her best to raise the life of her court to a level becoming to the new great power, mainly modelling it on France. But festivities and pleasures were by no means her only preoccupation. Many learned men of that age, among them Descartes, spent some time at her court, which under her tutelage became a centre for scientists, authors and artists. – The National Art Museums, Stockholm.

Sweden obtained not only Western Pomerania, with Rügen, Stettin and Wismar, but also the duchies of Bremen and Verden. She had become a great European power.

Ever since Breitenfeld, however, her armies had more and more come to consist of legionaries, until at the close of the Thirty Years War only some 20 per cent of the troops were still Swedes or Finns. The long war effort – modern research has shown – had exhausted the country's population. And few indeed of its many enlisted men who had been sent to the continent had ever come home. Economically, too, Sweden was on her knees. Poor and sparsely populated, she simply was not up to supporting the great power status which her armies, heavily subsidized by France and Holland, had gained for her. The Swedish empire, too, was a 'colossus with feet of clay'.

The seventeenth century, furthermore, had transformed Sweden into a military state, where everything had been progressively subordinated to the needs of the army and navy. Now that the war in Germany was over, these armies could neither be brought home, nor could the country have supported them if they had been. Even the officers' demands for remuneration for their exploits could not be met. So short of funds indeed was the Crown that at the 1650 Parliament there was a head-on confrontation between the aristocracy and the three other lower Estates: clergy, burghers and peasants – a clash which Queen Kristina – Gustav II Adolf's daughter – exploited to force through the election of her cousin, the Count Palatine Karl Gustav, as her successor. Four years later she herself abdicated, left the country, converted to the Catholic faith and settled in Rome.

At his succession in 1654 Karl X Gustav was faced with virtually insoluble problems, both in regard to the Crown's finances and of how to support the armies. His solution to both was to attack Poland. Opening in the summer of 1655, this campaign led to great initial successes. Warsaw and Cracow were taken and the King of Poland was forced to flee. But the Swedish occupation also unleashed a national resistance movement, and though, in July 1656, the Swedish army won a major victory outside Warsaw, it could only with difficulty maintain itself in the country. When Russia soon afterwards declared war, Karl X Gustav's position became untenable, the more so when, in 1657, Denmark, seeing a chance of avenging the 1645 Peace of Brömsebro and of regaining her domination over the Baltic, also declared war.

In this quandary Karl X Gustav decided to evacuate Poland and attack Denmark from the south. In the autumn of 1657 he seized the fortress of Fredriksodde, on the Little Belt, and occupied the whole of Jutland. His campaign was brought to a halt by Danish naval superiority; but aided by an unusually cold winter Karl X Gustav marched his army across the frozen Great

47

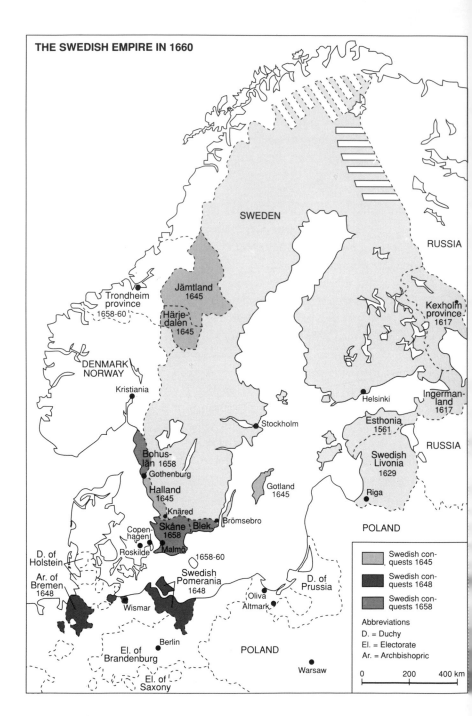

THE SWEDISH EMPIRE IN 1660

SWEDEN

RUSSIA

Jämtland
1645

Trondheim
province
1658-60

Härje-
dalen
1645

Kexholm
province
1617

DENMARK
NORWAY

Kristiania

Helsinki

Ingerman-
land
1617

Stockholm

Esthonia
1561

Bohus-
län 1658

Gothenburg

RUSSIA

Swedish
Livonia
1629

Halland
1645

Gotland
1645

Knäred

Riga

Copen-
hagen

Skåne Blek
1658

Brömsebro

POLAND

Roskilde

Malmö

1658-60

D. of
Holstein

Swedish
Pomerania
1648

D. of
Prussia

Ar. of
Bremen
1648

Wismar

Oliva

Altmark

Swedish con-
quests 1645

Berlin

El. of
Brandenburg

POLAND

Swedish con-
quests 1648

Swedish con-
quests 1658

Warsaw

Abbreviations
D. = Duchy
El. = Electorate
Ar. = Archbishopric

El. of
Saxony

0       200      400 km

The Swedish Empire in 1660
It was after the Peace of Westphalia in 1648 and the peace treaty with Denmark in 1658 that Sweden's empire reached its maximum extent. To her earlier annexations in the Baltic area had been added Pomerania and some smaller regions in northern Germany, all part of a plan to turn the Baltic into a Swedish sea, a *mare clausum*. Denmark, the main rival, was also being enveloped. These two ambitions, however, had to be abandoned. Two continental powers, Russia and Brandenburg, proved too strong. As early as 1660 the Baltic island of Bornholm and the province of Trondheim had to be returned to Denmark. More important to Sweden was to have retained Skåne and Bohuslän, thus providing the realm with a natural sea frontier to the south and west. Domination of the sea and overseas trade steadily gave way to preoccupation with the power of the national state.

Belt, threatened Copenhagen, and, in 1658, at Roskilde, dictated his own peace terms, under which Sweden got Skåne, Halland, Blekinge, Bornholm, Bohuslän, and the Norwegian province of Trondheim.

That autumn Karl X Gustav, with a view to conquering the whole of Denmark, again declared war. But the Dutch fleet came to the Danes' assistance, and in February 1660, Karl X Gustav, having failed to seize Copenhagen, suddenly died. Under a new peace treaty Bornholm and the province of Trondheim were returned to Denmark. But the other disputed provinces remained Swedish. In this way the Danish-Swedish frontier came to be what it still is.

Not that the Danes had given up all hope of reconquering Skåne, Halland and Blekinge. Upon Sweden becoming embroiled in the 1674 war between France and Brandenburg, Denmark returned to the attack and in June 1675 landed an army in Skåne. Though the young king Karl XI won a brilliant victory at Lund in December 1676, Danish troops continued to occupy large parts of Skåne, with heavy losses to both sides. Indeed this, the so-called Skåne War, was the most sanguinary of any fought between the two countries. Even so, upon France negotiating a new peace at Fontainebleau and Lund in 1679, the frontiers remained unchanged. Sweden had successfully defended her domination of the Baltic.

49

The Swedish man-of-war 'Svärdet' (The Sword) on fire and shot to pieces during the battle off the island of Öland on June 1, 1676, when the Danes almost totally destroyed the Swedish fleet. At the outset of the action the Swedish flagship 'Kronan' (The Crown) capsized, blew up, and sank with all hands. Found and recovered in the 1980s, its remains and equipment, together with its crew's possessions, are to be seen in Kalmar Museum. Together with the royal flagship 'Vasa', which in 1628 sank in Stockholm harbour when setting out on her maiden voyage and is now on view after being salvaged, they give a good idea of life on board a seventeenth-century Swedish man-of-war. – Bra Böcker Archives.

## Karl XII (Charles XII)

One of Sweden's chief problems during the 1611–1718 period was how to maintain the great armies she needed to support her position as a major power. During the first part of her imperial age, a period of uninterrupted warfare, they had supported themselves by fleecing and plundering enemy territories. It was only from 1660 onwards, after a more lasting state of peace had been reached, and during the Skåne War – the first to be waged within the realm itself – that the problem became overt. And it

50

was after the end of the Skåne War, between 1680 and 1690, that a new system was set up to cope with it.

Under this system, known as *indelningsverket*, commissioned and non-commissioned officers alike were allotted, in lieu of salary, Crown farms where they could support themselves in peacetime. At the same time the peasantry was divided up into *rotar*, recruitment units, each responsible for recruiting, equipping and supporting one soldier. Usually he, too, was given an outcropper's cottage and a cash grant toward the cost of his equipment. In this way a standing army was brought into being, capable of mobilization at short notice.

Ever since the Thirty Years War Swedish foreign policy had been based on the French alliance – the one which in 1674 had involved the country in the war with Brandenburg. But then the whole policy was rescinded. From 1680 onwards Sweden would ally herself with Britain and Holland, France's enemies, while at the same time escalating her conflict with Russia, where Peter the Great had adopted an active foreign policy, designed in part to break Sweden's grip on, and access to, the Baltic trade.

Upon the Elector of Saxony, Augustus II the Strong, being elected King of Poland in 1697, the Livonian aristocracy sought and obtained his support against Swedish policies in their province. At the same time Denmark, Poland and Russia formed an aggressive alliance, their plan being to launch simultaneous attacks on Sweden in February 1700.

Though Karl XI's death, three years previously, had left the Crown to his 15-year-old son, Sweden was well prepared to meet the aggression. To avoid the weaknesses inherent in a regency, the young Karl XII was immediately declared of age and invested with plenary powers. By now the country was strong, both economically and militarily.

Supported by the British and Dutch fleets, the new well-organized standing army immediately landed in Själland and, after a swift advance, extorted from Denmark, under the Peace of Traventhal, an undertaking not to support Sweden's enemies. After which, in that summer and autumn of 1700, the Swedish army was promptly shipped over to the eastern front, where Augustus II had opened his campaign by investing Riga, and Peter I and his Russians were attacking Narva. Turning first on his Russian foe, Karl XII in November 1700 won the brilliant victory of Narva, capturing and annihilating, despite its vast superiority in numbers, most of the Russian army.

Thereafter he attacked Augustus II's army, mostly Saxons, and by crossing the Dwina forced it to retreat. The ensuing Polish campaign (1702–06) culminated in several more Swedish victories, among them the one at Fraustadt. Under the Peace of Altranstadt (1706) Augustus II renounced the Polish throne and the anti-Swedish alliance was formally dissolved.

All that winter and spring (1706–07) Karl XII, lingering at Altranstadt, was courted by German princes and the great powers' diplomats. But though in the spring even the Duke of Marlborough came and tried to prevail on Karl XII to side with Britain and the Empire in the War of the Spanish Succession, Karl XII obstinately adhered to his own plan of attacking Russia, his sole remaining opponent in the Great Northern War.

In the summer of 1708, having occupied Poland in the previous year, he invaded Russia at the head of 40,000 men. At the same time a second Swedish army, 16,000 strong, set out from the Riga region, escorting a massive supply train. Before this smaller force could appear on the scene of action, however, it was utterly defeated and all the main army's supplies were lost. Meanwhile the Russians were ruthlessly setting fire to everything combustible in Karl XII's path; and since the winter of 1708–09 turned out to be exceptionally cold, the Swedish army found itself in an untenable position. Breaking off its advance on Moscow, Karl XII, hoping to find plentiful supplies and join forces with the hetman Mazeppa's rebellious troops, turned south toward the Ukraine. But on June 28, 1709, at the Battle of Poltava, his whole campaign ended in catastrophe. Tsar Peter's troops virtually wiped Karl XII's entire force, and a few days later, at Perevolotjna, even its remains had to surrender and were marched into captivity. Karl XII himself fled to Turkey, where for five long years he remained isolated at Bender, in Moldavia, close to the Turkish-Russian frontier, vainly trying to induce the Turks to attack Russia. Not until 1715, after a long and solitary ride across Europe, did he get home. Setting up his headquarters at Lund, he made every effort to rouse his subjects to renewed military efforts, his priority this time being to conquer Norway. In 1717, though he captured Kristiania (Oslo) after a brief

At the Battle of Poltava (June 28, 1709), the Swedish army was utterly defeated by the Russians. A few days before it was fought the hitherto always victorious Karl XII had been wounded in one foot. When his plan of attack failed and General Rehnskiöld, to whom he had handed over, was captured, the king, though lying on a stretcher, resumed command and carried out an orderly withdrawal. Even so, a few days later, the remains of the Swedish army, some 25,000 strong, capitulated at Perevolotjna. This defeat spelt the end of Sweden's military empire. – The Royal Library, Stockholm.

campaign, other Danish fortresses held out, and he had to relinquish it. Next year, renewing his campaign by investing the frontier fortress of Fredriksten, on November 30, 1718 he was shot through the head in the trenches – whether by an enemy bullet or an assassin's is still a matter of debate. But there is strong evidence for regicide.

Karl XII had never married, and behind the rumours of

Karl XII's dead body borne over the Swedish-Norwegian mountains. In this painting, inspired by hero worship, Gustaf Cederström (1845–1933) depicts the dead hero's last journey. No sooner had the king fallen in the trenches outside Fredriksten fortress (Nov 30, 1718) than the siege was raised and the campaign terminated. Fredrik of Hesse, the king's brother-in-law and chief lieutenant, took over command and among other things distributed the army's war chest among its officers. – The National Art Museums, Stockholm.

murder lay rival claims to the succession. So swiftly did the Crown Prince Fredrik of Hesse and his spouse, Karl XII's sister Ulrika Eleonora, act, everything suggests they had been expecting the king's death. Seizing power, the Hessian party had Ulrika Eleonora elected queen; and, in the following year (1720) her husband was elected king.

Meanwhile peace negotiations had been opened, and in the

settlement between Sweden, Denmark and such German states as had taken part in the war Sweden was obliged to relinquish all her German possessions except a small part of Pomerania. Under the Peace of Nystad (1721) she also lost all her Baltic provinces, as well as south-eastern Finland and the key fortress of Viborg, to Russia. Sweden was again a minor state.

# The Age of Freedom
# and the Gustavian
# Autocracy, 1719–1809

## A Parliamentary Constitution

Karl XII's death had precipitated a bloodless revolution, an almost total change in the mode of government. 'Here everyone is behaving like flies that have survived the winter and come to life again,' we read in a letter describing the political activity in Stockholm in December 1718. The prime issue was the succession. Under Karl XI's will, ratified by the Estates, women were entitled to succeed to the throne. In the event of the monarch having no male heir, it was to pass to his eldest unmarried daughter. But Karl XII's elder sister, Hedvig Sofia, wife of the Duke of Holstein-Gottorp, had died in 1708, and her young son Karl Fredrik of Holstein-Gottorp's prospects of asserting his rights were at best slender. Until her marriage to Fredrik of Hesse in 1715 Karl XII's younger sister, Ulrika Eleonora, on the other hand, had enjoyed an unquestioned right. But no matter how energetically Fredrik and his supporters asserted his wife's claim, the Estates, assembled in Stockholm in 1719, would not accept it. Only upon Ulrika Eleonora renouncing all claims to absolute power was she elected. Upon her trying next year to make her husband co-regent, she was instead obliged to abdicate in his favour. Even Fredrik I was only elected after further constitutional concessions.

At first, under the 1720 Constitution, supplemented with new parliamentary rules in 1723, the political centre of gravity lay in the Council, in which the king had to content himself with a mere two votes, plus a casting vote. And throughout the 1720s and

1730s the rule of the Council, strongly led by its Lord President, Arvid Horn, would be decisive.

But Parliament, too, was in a strong constitutional position. Meeting every third year, or oftener if it so wished, it alone controlled the state's finances and had exclusive control of legislation. And not only this. It also exerted its sway over foreign policy through its Secret Commission, and at any moment could also intervene in the administration or the judiciary.

Not until the session of 1738–39 would the latent opposition

'Happy Peasants' – oil painting from the mid-eighteenth century, now at the Nordic Museum, Stockholm. An idyllic picture of country life and the various activities on a Swedish farm. The text reads: 'An eight-cow peasant who has his horse God-fearing, honest, good neighbour too, short in one leg, friends with his clergyman, happy at his work, where he feels best of all.'

between the Council and Parliament come to a head. After judicial scrutiny of their actions, Arvid Horn's supporters on the Council were debarred from all parliamentary proceedings and Horn himself had to resign. For the future the Council's composition would be decided by parliamentary majority.

Opposition to Arvid Horn's régime had meanwhile given rise to a parliamentary party, known as the Hats, who were demanding a change in both domestic and foreign policies. After Horn's fall from power in 1738, his supporters formed another party, known originally to their opponents as the 'Nightcaps', but who in parliamentary contexts came to be known as the Caps.

It was in the struggle between these two parties that a political system developed, strongly reminiscent of contemporary parliamentary government in Britain. Even if in Sweden the councillors' political responsibility was heavily tied down by juridic

forms, Parliament had the right both to appoint them and decide over their policies. It is this parliamentary system of the Age of Freedom (1719–72) that has ever afterwards formed the basis of the Swedish tradition of political freedom.

## Agriculture

Sweden's period as a great power had drastically exploited both the country's economy and its population, more than 90 per cent of which still lived by agriculture and cattle-grazing. This exploitation had reached its climax in the famine years of the late 1690s and during the Great Northern War (1700–21), during which the plague of 1710–11 also claimed large numbers of victims. What things were like in the countryside in 1719 has

Illustration in a work dated 1749 'On the Improvement of Agriculture', by Petter Strandberg. It demonstrates the use of plough and harrow and offers suggestions for various sowing machines. The great obstacle to all attempts to rationalize Swedish agriculture lay in the many narrow individually owned strips of land making up each field. This too can be seen in the picture, published at the height of the debate on land reform. – Copper engraving by Jean Eric Rehn.

61

'View of Gothenburg from the Kämpe Quay', watercolour by Elias Martin,
1787. It is eloquent of the prosperity brought into Sweden by the far eastern
traffic. Right: the Swedish East India Company's big new building, now the
Gothenburg Museum, which still dominates this part of the city. The main
canal is packed with smaller vessels bringing in goods to be sold at auction
in the company's warehouse from East Indiamen anchored out in the roads.
Though most of the great cargoes of tea, porcelain, silk and spices imported
from China were reexported, the extensive profits stayed in Sweden. The
great access of risk capital thus created was of great importance to
eighteenth-century Sweden's flourishing condition, economic and cultural.
– The Gothenburg Museum.

been described by a Dutch traveller: 'Nowhere in Sweden did I see a single young man between 20 and 40 years of age, only soldiers. The cruel war had swept away almost the entire youth of this unhappy realm... The whole kingdom to an unbelievable degree [was] run to seed. Often, arriving at an inn, we found neither people nor horses.'

The good harvests of the 1720s and 1730s quickly changed all this, and throughout the rest of the eighteenth century conditions for agriculture were excellent. This led among other things to a sharp growth in population and the cultivation of much new land. The self-owning peasants were enriched by steadily rising prices for agricultural produce, and their tax burden, for the most part payable in cash, grew lighter with inflation.

As a result of the peasants' growing assets landownership changed significantly. Cultivators of Crown homesteads were able to purchase them at very favourable prices, and after such purchases had been regulated by law in 1723, many such former Crown lands became new sources of taxation. From having constituted about 30 per cent of the soil in 1700, the peasantry's homesteads would rise to be more than 50 per cent in 1800, aristocratic (non-taxable) land remaining unchanged at 33 per cent. Add to this that the peasantry had also begun buying up aristocratic lands (ever more extensively after it became legal for them to do so in 1789) and one realizes a basis had been laid for the peasantry's strong political position in the late nineteenth century.

At the same time gaps between social classes in the countryside were widening. More and more homesteads were having to be split up to provide for ever larger families. The available arable land not sufficing, the unpropertied class was becoming ever more numerous, until, from only forming a small fraction of the population, it became a majority – the upshot in the long run being the great landless proletariat which, in the nineteenth century, would become a major outcropper problem and result in mass emigration to the New World.

Eighteenth-century farming methods were also becoming

more efficient. One condition for these improvements was the so-called *storskiftet*. Whereas each farm in a village had hitherto owned and tilled a narrow strip of each field, the new arrangement, introduced as a result of a series of regulations in the 1757–62 period, reorganized the farm lands into larger units. Since each peasant's farm now consisted in principle of a single lot in each unit of arable or grazing land, this enabled him to decide for himself when he wished to sow and reap, or whether to cultivate his land differently from his neighbour.

Not that this amalgamation of smallholdings dissolved the village community. Only with the next great change, in the nineteenth century, when the land would successively be redistributed into separate, often widely separated farms, would that happen.

These new and more efficient possibilities were exploited in many places. This is to say that among the most important

agricultural innovations was a transition to rotational farming, something that greatly increased the yield. Such technical novelties as iron ploughs were also introduced, and conscious efforts were made to effectivize and modernize the country's agriculture by giving good advice and instruction. Between 1791 and 1817 these efforts would give birth to farming associations.

## Trade and Economy

Despite all her victories in the Thirty Years War and against Denmark, seventeenth-century Sweden, though an empire, had been a poor country, with economic resources far from adequate to support her status as a great military power, bequeathed to her by Gustav II Adolf's and Karl X Gustav's victorious campaigns.

An early eighteenth-century ironworks. Emanuel Swedenborg (1688–1772), mystic and mining engineer, attached this illustration, obtained from Germany, to a memorandum he presented to the 1723 Parliament and afterwards reprinted it in his great work on iron, De Ferro, 1734. But it also gives a good idea of the methods introduced into Swedish ironwork estates in the eighteenth century. In the foreground a smith is hammering out sheet iron that will be reheated and passed through a cutting machine, driven by a water-wheel (far right), from which power is transmitted to the rollers and cutter by cogs and axles.
– The Royal Library, Stockholm.

65

Carl von Linné (1707–78), known to the world as Linnaeus, was the most internationally famous of all eighteenth-century Swedish scientists. His *Systema Naturae*, published in 1735, was quickly recognized and his sexual system for plants became basic to botany. This portrait, painted by A. Roslin a few years before Linnaeus' death, was the one he preferred himself. As usual, he has his favourite flower, the Linnea, in his buttonhole. – The National Art Museums, Stockholm.

What had above all been lacking had been resources of fluid risk capital. Despite all attempts to create it via copper exports and various trading companies, the Swedish economy had remained what it had always been: almost totally a barter economy. Karl XI's system of military recruitment would help preserve large segments of this antiquated system for centuries to come. Even in the beginning of the next century Sweden was still a small and poverty-stricken society, on the very fringes of European civilization.

Yet only fifty years had to pass before Sweden, in the reign of Gustav III (1771–92), would reach the same commercial, scientific and cultural level as the most progressive countries of western and southern Europe. All over the continent such names as Christopher Polhem (engineer), Anders Celsius (astronomer and physicist), Carl Linnaeus (botanist), Emanuel Swedenborg (natural scientist and religious mystic) and Olof von Dalin (poet and publicist) were known and respected. Trade flourished. All kinds of newly established manufactures were in a state of swift growth and development. Both culturally and economically the eighteenth century – notably the 1720–90 period – is a great period in Sweden's history.

Such swift economic, scientific and cultural developments called for access to fluid risk capital, and this could not be come by except through commerce, notably of the transoceanic kind. Thus in all the arts and in culture generally, in science and in literature, we everywhere find an interest in, and influences from, China. Among many eminent concerns, one – the Swedish East India Company, founded in 1731 – stands out in this respect, as it also does in industry and economics. There is hardly an initiative that in some degree cannot be traced back to its head office in Gothenburg, which provided so much of the capital invested during the Age of Freedom and the Gustavian period. Practically every Swede then eminent in trade, manufactures or industry is to be found in the lists of its directors, supercargoes or investors.

Around the mid-century iron and steel and their products constituted about three-quarters of the country's total exports. The Bergslagen ironworks and iron manufactures were in a state of rapid expansion. At the same time the forests, hitherto mainly valuable as a source of charcoal for smelting iron and copper, were becoming steadily more important as more and more tar and timber were being exported. The exceptionally plentiful herring catches of the century's latter half also contributed to growing prosperity, particularly along or off the west coast.

Though only one new town was founded, the swift expansion in trade and manufactures were giving the town burghers ever greater influence. At the same time the middle classes' more eminent representatives were becoming steadily more numerous, and proprietors of ironworks estates were wielding extensive influence over the economy. Commoners were also occupying more and more positions in the administration. The whole century, in Sweden as elsewhere, was characterized by greater equality and social mobility.

During the Great Northern War (1700–21) and in the years immediately following it a great number of individuals were ennobled. The 1719 Parliament had also done away with the distinction between high and low aristocracy – greatly, of course, to the latter's advantage. And though the nobleman's exclusive aristocratic right to hold high office and exemption from land-tax were both confirmed in 1723, it was a privilege which could not be upheld in reality. So many commoners were in fact now being appointed to high office and acquiring tax-exempt estates and farms that, in 1789, both these and other aristocratic privileges would be formally abolished. Not however before they, during the Age of Freedom, had aggravated the class conflicts which, in 1772, would put an end to the powers of the Estates.

## Party Politics in the Age of Freedom

The peace treaties of 1720–21 having reduced Sweden to the level of a second-rate power, Arvid Horn's government had thereafter pursued cautious policies and chiefly taken refuge in good relations with Britain and neutrality in great power conflicts.

Such policies, however, were less and less to the liking of the group of young men, mostly new aristocrats, who in the 1730s formed a majority in the House of Nobility. The aristocracy had strong cultural links with France. And it was thirsting to avenge Poltava. This policy, around which gathered the parliamentary party that would become known as the Hats, was also supported by a group of influential merchants from the burgher Estate. Favoured by current prosperity, they wanted a mercantilist economic policy, with high tariffs and strong state support to protect their fledgling manufactures.

Having gained a majority at the 1738–39 Parliament, it was the Hats who forced Arvid Horn to resign, replacing him as Lord President of the Council by Carl Gyllenborg, the radical Hats' leader in the House of Nobility. And indeed the Secret Commission had already obliged the Council to change its foreign policy and among other things sign a ten-year treaty of friendship with France.

The outbreak in 1740 of the War of the Austrian Succession, with France and Prussia on one side and Austria, Britain and the Netherlands on the other, gave the Hat party hawks the upper hand at the 1740–41 Parliament. France promised lavish subsidies, and in March 1741 war was declared on Russia.

This, the Hats' war of 1741–43, ended in defeat and a Russian occupation of Finland. At the peace negotiations, Fredrik I being childless, the question of the succession arose again. Russia supported the candidature of Adolf Fredrik of Holstein-Gottorp – grandson of Charles XII's elder sister and native of a country closely allied to Russia – and it was only by electing him heir to the throne that Sweden, in 1743, could sign the Peace of Åbo, under which only part of south-east Finland was lost to Russia.

This defeat, however, did not cost the Hats their power. In many ways they even became stronger, as a result of the mid-century's economic growth, despite inflation, and because of the cultural influences flowing in from the French Enlightenment.

In 1757, the French alliance embroiled Sweden in yet another armed conflict: the so-called Seven Years War (1756–63), now against Prussia. This time Swedish involvement only amounted to a few minor fights in Pomerania. Nor did the peace, signed at Hamburg in 1762, redraw the frontier between Swedish Pomerania and Prussia.

What this expensive war in Pomerania did unleash, however, was a wave of criticism of the Hat government; and the 1765 Parliament forced it to resign. The policies of the younger Caps, who now took over, differed totally from those of the past twenty-five years. At home they instigated a ruthless deflation, restricted credit, were sparing with state funds, reduced customs dues protecting manufactures, and swept away a host of regulations. Abroad, Sweden broke with the French treaty and, replacing it with a similar one with Britain, made approaches to Russia.

But the Cap régime was of brief duration. Ousting them from

the Council at the 1769 Parliament, the Hats formed a new government.

Meanwhile the whole political scene had been deeply split by antagonism between the aristocracy and the three other Estates. Upon the latter, at the 1771–72 Parliament, joining hands to restrict aristocratic privileges, the aristocracy turned for support to the young Gustav III, who in 1771 had succeeded his father Adolf Fredrik.

It was this situation that Gustav III, on August 19, 1772, exploited to carry out a coup d'état. Using the military to force the Estates to relinquish their powers, he imposed on them a new constitution that in all essentials reintroduced the 'sovereignty principle' – i.e. the king's exclusive right to rule – and again reduced the Council to merely advisory status. On the other hand Parliament retained power over taxation as well as a certain legislative influence. Basically, however, Gustav III had replaced the parliamentary government of the Age of Freedom with his own royal autocracy.

## The Gustavian Age, 1772–1809

*Där låg ett skimmer över Gustafs dagar,*
*fantastiskt, utländskt, flärdfullt om du vill,*
*men det var sol däri, och, hur du klagar,*
*var stodo vi, om de ej varit till?*
*All bildning står på ofri grund till slutet,*
*blott barbarit var en gång fosterländskt;*
*men vett blev plantat, järnhårt språk blev brutet,*
*och sången stämd och livet mänskligt njutet,*
*och vad Gustaviskt var blev därför även svenskt.*


A sheen there was on Gustaf's day,
fantastic, foreign, frivolous, you say?
Complain as we will, the sun shone then;
where were we now had it never been?

70

All culture stands on unfree soil;
native barbarism was our all.
But sense, once planted, broke its iron tongue;
the singer found his note, and life was young,
Gustavian all Swedish things became.

In his poem on the occasion of the Swedish Academy's half-centenary in 1836, the poet Esaias Tegnér fixed what has seemed to posterity to be the essential quality of the Gustavian Age: as a first flowering of the country's culture, admittedly in line with that of the rest of Europe and notably of France – albeit in the specifically Swedish version known simply as 'Gustavian'.

When his father, King Adolf Fredrik, died in 1771, Crown Prince Gustav was visiting Paris. The immense scientific, liter-

Johan Tobias Sergel's (1740–1814) statue of Gustav III is one of the sculptor's most important works, modelled in the king's last years, but not finished until after his assassination in 1792. Based on the Apollo Belvedere it is expressive of the great sculptor's devotion to his patron and admiration for all he had done for the arts and culture. Sergel himself said he wanted to depict the king as 'the most enlightened monarch and the most loyal to his friends the earth had produced'.
– Photo: Gösta Glase.

71

ary, artistic and architectural impressions the city made on him would set their stamp on all his subsequent actions. Not that he was the only Swede to subscribe to the Enlightenment. The aristocracy, the upper échelons of the bourgeoisie, prosperous merchants, craftsmen and other townspeople were familiar with the writings of Voltaire, Montesquieu and Rousseau. Many homes were buying and reading French and English as well as Swedish authors.

The first great Swedish literary figure of the age was the poet Olof von Dalin, who had begun publishing his newspaper *Then Swänska Argus* in 1732. He had his mid-century followers in such poets as Gustav Philip Creutz and Gustaf Fredrik Gyllenborg. But only in the Gustavian Age does Swedish poetry finally burst into bloom, with the immortal songs of Carl Michael Bellman and the prose and poetry of Johan Henrik Kellgren,

'My daughter's portrait', oil painting by Pehr Hilleström, evidences the swift growth of literary interests in eighteenth-century Sweden. The role played by the French Enlightenment is stressed by the presence of Voltaire's bust in the background. – The Royal Library, Stockholm.

Carl Gustaf Leopold and Anna Maria Lenngren. It was this flowering which, in 1786, would motivate Gustav III to found the Swedish Academy.

The other arts, too, were in their prime. Painters like Carl Gustaf Pilo, Alexander Roslin, Adolf Ulrik Wertmüller and Carl Fredrik von Breda were also working abroad and enjoyed international fame. The achievements of the sculptor Tobias Sergel and the architect Carl Hårleman reveal how eminent a position in European culture Sweden had suddenly attained to. So do the many elegant manor houses and other eighteenth-century buildings, not to mention such crafts as those of Swedish silversmiths and cabinet makers.

Gustav III's policies during the first decade of his reign largely followed those of the reforming younger Caps. Thus the 1766 Freedom of the Press Act was replicated by another in 1774. Many restrictions on free trade were abolished and the penal system was made more humane. Ever since the Reformation the State Lutheran Church had had an exclusive care of souls; but in 1781 religious freedom was introduced for foreigners and in 1782 special regulations permitted Jews to settle and practice their religion in all major towns. In 1777 the economy's international position was strengthened by devaluing the *riksdaler*. All these measures, as well as his singular passion for theatre, caused Gustav III to be seen, and rightly, as one of Europe's most enlightened monarchs.

But the 1780s brought growing tensions between him and the opposition. As the king grew more despotic, the aristocracy, influenced by French libertarian ideas, again began demanding more influence. At the 1786 Parliament the opposition, in a majority, restricted its grants of money to the Crown and threw out several royal bills.

Gustav III was not only a cultural but also a political franco-phile. The opposition had attached itself to pro-Russian interests. Seeing in this a means of regaining his – initially immense – popularity the king now adopted a more aggressive foreign policy, and in 1788 attacked Russia, with a view to regaining the

Finnish provinces lost under the treaties of Nystad (1721) and
Åbo (1743). The war, mostly fought at sea, ended after the
indecisive battle of Hogland and a Swedish naval victory at
Svensksund. The Peace of Värälä (1790) made no change in the
Finnish frontiers.

Shortly after the war's outbreak in 1788 some Swedish
aristocratic officers who had objected to Gustav III's aggression
as unconstitutional had formed the so-called Anjala League and
mutinied. Gustav III summoned Parliament, and in February
1789 by means of an Act of Union and Security carried out a new
coup d'état. This established a total autocracy and abolished
such crucial aristocratic privileges as the sole right to own tax-
free land and occupy the higher positions in the state.

Among an aristocracy affected by ideas of the sovereignty of the nation simultaneously exploding in the French Revolution the king's high-handed behaviour unleashed a virulent opposition, and in March 1792 Gustav III was severely wounded in an assassination attempt during a masked ball in his own opera house and died two weeks later.

The fortress of Sveaborg, on seven rocky islets outside Helsinki. Begun in 1748 and complete in 1772, it was intended to be the main base of the Swedish archipelago fleet in the Gulf of Finland, and 'point d'appui' for an assault on Russia. But on May 3, 1808, during the Finnish War, it was besieged by Russian troops and capitulated without a fight, doing much to bring about the disastrous Swedish defeat and loss of Finland. This oil painting, showing the fortress under construction, is by Admiral Augustin Ehrensvärd, who not only created it but was also a talented artist. – The National Art Museums, Stockholm.

The plot miscarried politically, though, and the reign of his son and successor Gustav IV Adolf (1796–1809) would also be a period of royal autocracy. Its policies, however, were dictated to a great degree by the wars of the French Revolution and Napoleon. Crucial to Gustav IV Adolf's foreign policy was his personal objection to both. In 1805 this led to Sweden joining the disastrous Third Coalition. The victorious Napoleonic armies quickly overran Swedish Pomerania and in 1807 the French and Russian emperors signed the Treaty of Tilsit, which among other things stipulated that Sweden must break with Britain and join the Continental System. Since this would have cut off her vital trade with Britain, Sweden refused, whereupon Russia attacked in Finland.

The war of 1808–09 ended in total defeat for the Swedish army, and Russia occupied not only the whole of Finland, but even part of northern Sweden.

In March 1809, however, even before the war was over, Gustav IV Adolf had been deposed. The coup had been staged by most of the officer corps and such younger civil servants from the aristocratic opposition as were demanding constitutional government. Parliament was summoned, and worked out and adopted a new constitution. Based partly on Montesquieu's ideas, partly on indigenous experiences from the Age of Freedom and the Gustavian monarchy, the 1809 Constitution distributed power between king, Council and Parliament. Shortly afterwards Gustav III's younger brother was elected king, as Karl XIII. Sweden was now a constitutional monarchy.

# Sweden in the Nineteenth Century

# The First Bernadotte – and a New Foreign Policy

Karl XIII was childless. So once again it was a question of the succession, and again it was closely linked to foreign affairs.

Immediately after the coup, in 1809, a Danish prince, Kristian August of Augustenborg, was elected Crown Prince, a choice dictated by hopes of a united Sweden-Norway being able to remain neutral in the Napoleonic wars. But less than a year later he died. A successor had to be elected, which reopened the whole foreign policy issue in all its complexity.

That summer of 1810 Napoleon was at the height of his power. Having utterly defeated Austria and Prussia, he had forced Russia, by the Treaty of Tilsit, into his Continental System. Though it excluded her goods from Europe, Britain, however, had been victorious at sea, and still escaped him, and she responded by blockading France and all her allies, a measure which also cut France off from her remaining colonies.

Neither France nor Britain could tolerate the neutrality which Sweden had tried to adopt after her defeat in 1809. In May 1810 Napoleon demanded that she should break off relations with Britain and join the Continental System. A refusal would mean war. She could no longer remain neutral.

It was in this situation that the French marshal Jean Baptiste Bernadotte, son of a lawyer at Pau in the Pyrenees, was elected Crown Prince. A choice forced through by the francophile party, it seemed to take for granted that Sweden would ally herself with

Napoleon, with whose help it now became the goal of her foreign policy to regain Finland.

No sooner had Bernadotte – or Crown Prince Karl Johan, as he now was – landed in Sweden than he adopted quite another policy. His first important decision was to make approaches to Russia; and during his negotiations with the Tsar's emissary in December 1810 he repeatedly assured him that neither in the short nor the long run would he try to reconquer Finland. On the other hand Karl Johan expressed irritation with Denmark, asserting that the Norwegians would be happy to unite their country with Sweden. As he saw it, Sweden had common

Karl XIV Johan, as the Napoleonic marshal Jean Baptiste Bernadotte. This copper engraving by P.M. Alix, based on a drawing by H. le Dru, was distributed in 1810 to Members of Parliament on the eve of their election of a successor to the throne. It was intended to show him as a youthful man of action, allude to his military qualifications and stress his attachment to the ideas of the French Revolution, in all of which it unquestionably succeeded. – Bra Böcker Archives.

natural frontiers with Norway, which he hinted he hoped to acquire.

This union became the goal of his foreign policy, and already, in 1810–11, he tried to get both Russia to acquiesce and France to support him in forcing Denmark, then a French ally, to hand over Norway to Sweden. At the same time, however, tension between Napoleon and Tsar Alexander was growing fast, and a new Franco-Russian war was clearly in the offing. It was in this situation that Karl Johan, in the autumn of 1811, opened extremely secret negotiations with Britain.

His final decision, however, did not come until 1812. In January of that year French troops had occupied Swedish Pomerania. Its Swedish officials were replaced by Frenchmen, state property was confiscated and Swedish officers and soldiers were taken to France as prisoners of war.

This action unleashed strong reactions in Sweden. Nor did she delay her counter-measures. Whilst France was merely asked for an explanation, a Swedish initiative opened negotiations with Russia and Britain for a new anti-French alliance. It had been Napoleon's occupation of Pomerania which had precipitated a reversal of Swedish foreign policy.

These negotiations with Russia bore swift fruit. In April, Karl Johan, who ever since his arrival in Sweden had effectively been at the helm of state, formed a treaty of alliance with Russia. This was confirmed at a personal meeting between Crown Prince Karl Johan and Tsar Alexander at Åbo after Napoleon, on Midsummer Day 1812, had crossed the Niemen with overwhelming forces. In the spring of 1813, after the Grand Army had perished in the snows, a similar treaty was signed with Britain, and in May Karl Johan landed a Swedish army in Germany to take part in the new campaign against Napoleon.

In July its three leaders – the Tsar, King Fredrik Wilhelm of Prussia, and Crown Prince Karl Johan (Austria was still neutral) met at Trachenberg Castle in Silesia, and its outlines were drawn up. The allied armies were to operate in three major groups. Karl

80

Johan was to command the Army of the North, no fewer than 158,000 strong.

After Napoleon's defeat at the Battle of Leipzig, Karl Johan turned against Denmark, and after a very brief conflict obliged her to sign the Treaty of Kiel (January 14, 1814), under which the King of Denmark ceded Norway to Karl XIII and his successors. Norway was to be a separate kingdom, under the Swedish Crown. Karl Johan, it seemed, had achieved his goal.

But the Norwegians thought otherwise. On May 17, 1814, their representatives who had met at Eidsvoll and adopted a constitution of their own, elected the Danish prince Kristian Fredrik as their own king and demanded full national autonomy.

After a brief campaign against southern Norway that summer, Karl Johan forced the Norwegian Parliament to accept a union with Sweden, while at the same time promising to accept the Eidsvoll Constitution, with only such reservations as were inherent in a union. Norway became a kingdom, united with Sweden under the Swedish Crown, but with her own constitution and a fully autonomous domestic administration.

After the fall of Napoleon, which also put paid to any hopes Karl Johan had entertained of playing a future part in French affairs, his alliance with Alexander became the king-pin of his foreign policy. Though never popular with his subjects, it turned out well, and was in fact the beginning of the policy of peaceful neutrality which has characterized Swedish foreign policy ever since.

# Social Change and Industrialization

From the earliest times Sweden had always been sparsely populated. Up to about 1800 population growth had been slow, despite a birth rate more than double what it is today. Mortality, particularly infant mortality, had always been very high indeed, and in years of failed harvests, war or plague it had temporarily reduced the population.

But from the turn of the new century all this changed, and the population grew swiftly. Around 1800 it stood at 2.4 millions, but in 1850 it would be 3.5 millions, and in 1900 over 5.1 millions. Despite some 850,000 young Swedes emigrating to the New World between 1840 and 1900, the century more than doubled the population.

The poet Esaias Tegnér pithily summed up the reasons for this great change in the words 'peace, vaccination and potatoes'. Throughout the century Swedes were spared the mortality rates of its predecessors. Food was more plentiful as a result of potato crops and efficient grain farming, and this improved health, while smallpox vaccination, other medical progress and, above all, better hygiene reduced mortality. Since the birth rate did not fall, the population rose sharply.

Mostly it lived off agriculture. When the century began, over 90 per cent lived in the countryside. Only at a late date, compared with other West European countries, i.e. at the end of the nineteenth century, did industrialization really begin. Even in 1900 more than 50 per cent of Swedes were still farmers.

Scanian villagers assembled on the eve of the great land reform under which the old villages would be split up and their inhabitants scattered. (Kulturen, Lund.) Ever since the early Middle Ages the village had been the primary social unit. All important decisions had been made collectively in its assembly, and all work done in common. But during the nineteenth century farms came everywhere to be built on their own lands, often far from any neighbour. The village working teams were dissolved, each peasant now being free to organize work as he saw fit on his own farm. At the same time vast areas of new arable land came to be cultivated, and the Swedish countryside assumed its modern aspect. – Photo: IBL.

83

Both agriculture and the aspect of the country changed as a result of the so-called *laga skiftet*, under which the old villages were split up, and with them the working communities, as well as such meadowlands and outlying areas as had so far not been modified. This gave each homestead a single unified area, in many cases lying far out from the original centre. The country thus came to be covered with detached farms, many of them remote from the former villages, and each standing on its own land. At the same time the arable areas were vastly increased, more than tripling between 1810 and 1870.

Despite this immense cultivation of new land, Swedish agriculture could not in the long run absorb the swiftly growing population. Total yield, namely, was nothing like in proportion, partly because crops from the outlying areas were not as good as those from the older, more fertile ones; and partly because the period saw no corresponding expansion in other branches of agriculture, e.g. cattle breeding, which in some places even dwindled.

But redistribution of the land also had other effects besides its increased cultivation. The old villages had not only been occupied by farmers but also by outcroppers and cottagers. These latter, though owning no share of the village's ploughed lands, had usually had access to its common grazing lands and taken timber and firewood from its forests. The redistribution of common lands made it much harder for them to provide for themselves, thus widening the rural class gap, a development aggravated by other factors. Normally, self-owning farmers tried to keep their farm intact on the death of its owner, usually by passing it on to the eldest son. This is why the peasant class did not grow as fast as the rural population as a whole. Whilst the nineteenth century only saw it grow by one-third, the landless population was doubled. Thus land redistribution and population growth together gave rise to an ever larger class of poor and landless people.

Here we have the background to the great emigration which started seriously in the later 1860s and reached its apogée in the

1880s. In the 1880s alone 347,000 emigrants left Sweden, most to settle in North America, and for the fifty years between 1865 and 1914 the total was almost a million. Only from Ireland and Norway, among West European countries, was the exodus relatively greater.

In USA the Swedes settled in districts whose climate and

A steamship carrying emigrants to the New World puts out from Gothenburg – woodcut from a family magazine, 1887. It was in the 1880s emigration from Sweden reached its maximum. Similar scenes were almost daily occurrences in Gothenburg. – The Gothenburg Museum.

nature resembled their own. That is why most Swedish-Americans are to be found in the Middle West, notably Minnesota, and in the state of Washington, in the north-west. The emigration of so large a part of the population has given a great many Swedes links with friends and relatives in USA, and thus helped to

Karl XIV Johan inspecting works on the Göta Canal, in company with representatives of government and Parliament. Water-colour by A.C. Wetterling, 1856. To the king's left is Baltzar von Platen, whose idea it had been and who was chiefly responsible for its implementation. The building of the canal, which started in 1810 and was completed in 1832, occupied

maintain good relations and cultural collaboration between the two countries.

Iron production had long been Sweden's sole important industry. Yet almost throughout the nineteenth century it retained its centuries-old semi-craft and guild-like character and

upwards of 7,000 men. It was the first step in the development of communications within the country which would result in railways in the century's second half. Major public works were highly typical of nineteenth-century Sweden and provided the basis for the country's late but swift industrialization. – The National Art Museums, Stockholm.

ancient working patterns. Not until 1859 were the last of the government regulations that had so long dictated its economy removed, and not until the 1870s did more modern forms of organization begin to be introduced. Most of the important metal and engineering industry that today so largely sets its stamp on the country's output did not come into being until the decades just before the First World War.

Of even later date is the autonomous timber and timber products industry whose output for a while would dominate exports and which is still so important. As we have seen, the vast forests' earlier use had mostly been as a source of charcoal for the iron industry. As late as 1854 it was estimated that four to

From the mid-nineteenth century onwards the Swedish engineering industry began to develop. New factories were set up, ever more rapidly in the century's second half, above all in Stockholm and Gothenburg. In the bigger ones steampower was transmitted by a system of cogs and belts suspended from the roof. – Lithograph by G. Pabst, 1875.

five times as much timber was used for charcoal as was being exported. But it was also then, in the 1850s, that the introduction of the steam saw created new potential for the sawmills industry. Further, the introduction of free trade in Britain had just opened up markets for timber exports. Between 1850 and 1870 Swedish exports of sawn and planed timber products more than quadrupled.

The next great change came with the growth, around 1900, of the pulp industry. Here developments were even swifter. During the twenty years between 1894 and 1914 the Swedish pulp industry grew ten times over, one of the factors that made Sweden, in 1914, the world's largest exporter of timber products.

For a long while the country's sparse population and great geographical expanses hindered the development of modern communications. Not until Parliament in 1854 had decided that the state should build the mainlines did they become the basis of a nationwide network. During the 1860s and 1870s the first of them were opened between Stockholm, Gothenburg and Malmö – a very late development compared with other countries. In the USA the first railways had begun to be built around 1830, and by 1860 they were already 49,277 km in extent, or three times as much as in Sweden today. At that time the Swedish system totalled a mere 527 km.

It was in the 1890s and first decade of the twentieth century that the metals and engineering industries, which in their modern forms are so typical of today's Sweden, began to develop. The swift industrialization characteristic of that period began to reduce emigration. At the same time the towns were quickly expanding. Sweden was on the way to becoming an industrial country.

Parallel with the economic and social changes and the industrial revolution came cultural and political reforms. Their basic condition was general obligatory elementary education, introduced in 1842.

Typical of Swedish life are the popular movements which

from the mid-nineteenth century have been so important, culturally, politically and economically. Many of these had their roots, during the first part of the nineteenth century, in the form of 'associations', led by upper-class individuals in order to rectify obvious evils. The first popular mass organization formed under this head consisted of the non-conformist associations, formed in opposition to the spiritual oppression of the Lutheran State Church. Another was the teetotal association which, besides opposing the widespread drunkenness, would play a big part in educating the population. During the century's latter half a trade union and workers' political movement grew up, based above all on German and Danish models, and, in the twentieth century, would become more politically important than in most comparable countries. The Co-operative movement, too, did much to improve the individual's economy, especially among the less well-situated. Less political, but gradually no less comprehensive, was the sports movement, which gained wide support. In our own time it is these and other great popular movements which in so high degree have set their stamp on Swedish society.

The Swedish Fort Gustav defending the entrance to the harbour of the town of Gustavia, capital of the Swedish colony of Saint Barthélemy in the Leeward Islands in the Lesser Antilles group of the West Indies. Colonized by the French in 1648, the island was acquired by Sweden in 1784 in exchange for a French trading depot in Gothenburg. Less than 10 sq. miles (25 km²) in size, the little island has today c. 2,500 inhabitants. It remained Swedish until 1878 when it was sold to France for 320,000 francs. Gustavia, which still bears many traces from its period as a Swedish colony, was named after Gustav III. – Bra Böcker Archives.

## Conservatism *vs.* Liberalism

The general economic crisis after the Napoleonic wars had struck Sweden very hard. The war had brought violent inflation, favouring the peasantry but badly hurting wage-earners and small savers. True, after 1812 prices had stabilized and wages risen. But the balance of trade was deeply in the red and the

Swedish currency went on falling on the Hamburg exchange, which dominated in the north.

Karl Johan regarded this ever more adverse exchange rate – i.e. the krona's falling value – as the root cause of the country's economic difficulties. Therefore financial policy after 1815 was primarily directed against it, and his government did its best to keep up the value of the krona by supportive purchases. Despite great sacrifices, both on his own part and the state's, his policy did not work. The krona went on falling and Sweden fell ever deeper into the red, until in the end Karl Johan reluctantly had to accept the economic realities of his adoptive country's poverty and negative trade balance. In 1834 the krona was radically devalued. Only then did the Swedish economy become stabilized and the trade cycles improve.

The constitution adopted after the 1809 coup d'état had been based on Montesquieu's theories of a division of powers and on the long-standing oppositional claim that the nation should itself decide what taxes it would pay. Absolute monarchy, abolished in 1809, had been replaced with a constitutional monarchy. According to the new constitution the king could only exert his powers under the supervision of responsible councillors.

From the very outset Karl Johan, despite his middle-class origins and a career based on the French Revolution, had found it hard to swallow these constitutional restrictions on his own power. Even as Crown prince he had clashed with the most independently minded of his councillors. And as King Karl XIV Johan (1818–44) he chose them to an ever greater extent from among loyal bureaucrats who made no fuss about obeying orders.

Throughout his reign his policies were extremely conservative. Opposition demands for liberal reforms were rejected out of hand. And as the years went on his autocratic ways became ever more obvious. The aristocratic Magnus Brahe, his favourite and adjutant-general, was his personal adviser, and not merely the Council but even Karl Johan's only son and heir to the throne, Prince Oskar, had to turn to Brahe to gain the king's ear. In the 1830s, though liberal demands for reform were growing ever louder, it was this 'Brahe' or 'bedchamber régime' – so-called because of the king's habits as a late riser – which set its stamp on his rigidly conservative government. Every parliament was a head-on clash. In the intervals the king fought an ever bigger and more vocal liberal press by suppressing newspapers and prosecuting its publishers. Not until in his last years – after 1840 – would he yield on important points of reform.

A first condition for a more constitutional kind of government was the so-called departmental reform, passed by Parliament in 1840. This meant that each member of the Council became responsible for his own department, whose task was to prepare government business. It was this reform, so desired by liberals, that thereafter made it impossible for the king to deal with administrative matters without even informing his councillors. In the long run it would strengthen government at the expense of the royal authority.

Back in the 1830s Crown Prince Oskar had become a protagonist of social reform and great hopes were being placed in him. In liberal circles he was known as 'The Future'.

Constitutionally he was of another mind. When he ascended the throne in 1844 his power was still only formally limited by his councillors, whom he furthermore, like his father, appointed without consulting Parliament. He exploited, however, this strong position of the Crown on behalf of quite different policies.

The care of the poor was one of nineteenth-century Sweden's great problems, and after Oskar I's succession its reform was one of the most important points on the new government's agenda. The 1847 Poor Law declared now that 'it was incumbent upon each parish and town to feed its own poor'. This was the first time society's social obligations had ever been specifically stated in law.

One field of social policy which Oskar I was personally interested in was prisons and prisoner-care. In his own book *On*

93

The inventor John Ericsson, 1803–89. Autodidact and jack of all trades, his career began as a student engineer working on the Göta Canal. In 1826 he emigrated to Britain and in 1839 to the USA. Though his most important inventions were his propellors, he is best known for his ironclad warship 'The Monitor' whose rotating gun turret was epoch-making for naval warfare and had a crucial effect on the outcome of the Civil War in the USA. – The Royal Library, Stockholm.

*Punishments and Prisons* he described conditions in prisons and objected strongly to humiliating public punishments and proposed a cell system. He was one of the first to plead for humane treatment of prisoners. His book appeared during the 1840s in Norwegian, German, English, French, Dutch and Italian translations. In this way both Oskar I himself and Sweden came to be in the lead in working toward prison reforms far beyond the country's own frontiers.

Another field where Sweden led liberal reforms and the king made a great contribution was equal rights for women. The first step was to establish women's inheritance rights. The bill, presented by liberals in 1845 and supported by the three lower Estates, ran into stiff aristocratic resistance. In this situation the king's attitude was decisive. A second step in the same direction, taken in 1858, was to establish the unmarried woman's right to become legally responsible at the age of 25.

But the most important of all his reign's liberal reforms was the abolition of the guild system, in 1846. Hitherto the guilds had enjoyed a monopoly of their occupations. Now they were replaced by factory and crafts associations, open to all. Nor was trade any longer to be restricted to towns. For the first time since the towns had come into existence in the Middle Ages craftsmen and traders were now free to work in the countryside.

His reign (1844–59) was a period of many novelties: railways, telegraph, postage stamps and the decimal system were among them. Oskar I personally supported many new ideas and inventions. One example:

The first half of the nineteenth century in Sweden was the great age of canal building, notably of the Göta Canal, linking up the great lakes between Gothenburg and the Baltic. The railways, built in the 1830s and 1840s, were chiefly thought of as complements to them. They were to run from mines and industries to the nearmost canal, for further transport by water. Oskar I was one of the first to realize that the future lay with railways, and it was with his energetic support that the 1854 and 1856 Parliaments decided to build state-owned mainlines. This created an infrastructure that made possible the country's swift industrialization in the century's last decades.

Prime among liberal reforms during its first half was the demand for parliamentary reform: i.e. for abolition of the Four Estates system, with all its built-in aristocratic privileges. Not merely was it regarded as out of date and inequitable as a form of representation; it was seen as an obstacle to all real reform, as such. Though many proposals were made how to replace it, all were blocked by powerful vested interests, demanding their share of any new system.

Even so it was the last period of the Estates of the Realm that, no matter how heavily the older system was criticized, saw the harvest of liberal reforms: freedom of religion (1860), local government (1862), a new penal law (1864), free trade (1865) – all crowned by the parliamentary reform of 1866.

The parliamentary system finally adopted had been worked out by the Minister of Justice, Louis De Geer. Parliament was now to consist of two equal chambers. The differences in the manner of their election, however, limitations on franchise and eligibility, created differences between them. Members of the

Crowds cheering outside the House of Nobility on Dec 7, 1865, at the news that the nobility had accepted the parliamentary reform bill, i.e. the introduction of a two-chamber Parliament. For more than fifty years the abolition of the old four-estate system had been a major item in the Liberals' reform programme. – Drawing in *Ny Illustrerad Tidning*, 1865. The Royal Library, Stockholm.

First Chamber, which was supposed to provide for continuity and upper-class influence, were to be elected for nine years by the county councils and the major municipal councils and renewed successively by one-ninth annually. A candidate had to be 35 years old and have a big income or fortune. The Second Chamber was to be directly elected. Both franchise and eligibility were more easily accessible, particularly in what concerned property ownership, even if the regulations in this respect hardly seem democratic in our eyes. The upshot was that the First Chamber became a forum for estate-owners, high officials, wealthy city merchants and industrialists, and the Second came to consist of self-owning farmers, who formed the *Lantmanna-partiet*, or Rural Party.

This meant that Swedish politics got stuck in a kind of trench warfare between the two chambers. The First Chamber's demand for a stronger defence and an extended administration proved incompatible with the Second Chamber's demand for strict economy, its refusal to grant funds and its insistent demand for the abolition of land taxes. All reform bills were blocked by antagonisms between the two chambers.

Not until 1892 could a compromise be reached, and solutions found for the fiscal and defence issues. At the Prime Minister E.G. Boström's proposal it was decided to phase out land taxes and introduce a new military system. This latter was followed up by a Defence Act of 1901 that definitively put an end to the old *indelningsverket*, dating from the days of Karl XI, and introduced a conscript army, with a 240-day conscription period.

New questions had arisen, however, during the 1880s. Agriculture was in crisis as a result of a fall in world grain prices. Peasant demands for protective tariffs to keep up prices were supported by representatives of growing industries that were initially finding it hard to compete with older and better established industries elsewhere in Europe. In 1888 customs tariffs

Erik Gustaf Boström was prime minister 1891–1900 and 1902–1905. His strong position derived from his solutions to the land-tax and defence reforms at the extraordinary Parliament in 1892. His remarkable ability to find compromises and get opponents to agree to them earned him the sobriquet 'the state politician'. But in the Union question he was an extreme Swedish nationalist, and this terminated his premiership in 1905.
– The Royal Library, Stockholm.

were introduced for grain and certain industrial products, and in the years following they were extended.

But the tariff issue had split the Rural Party, so long dominant in the Second Chamber. There were also growing demands for universal and equal franchise, which unleashed extraparliamentary demonstrations, e.g. the so-called People's Parliaments of the 1890s. The workers' movement was growing ever stronger, and in 1889 it became politically organized by the founding of the Social Democratic Party. This in turn gave rise to political organizations, both in and outside Parliament. In 1900 the parliamentary Liberal Party was formed, and from 1902 had a national organization. To support the parliamentary Conservative parties a similar organization, the General Electoral Association, came into being in 1904. These were to be the fundaments of the political parties still dominating Swedish politics today.

## From Alliance to Neutrality

After 1812 Sweden's foreign policy had been overshadowed by the Holy Alliance, dominated by the Austrian chancellor Metternich and the Russian tsars. Liberals were strongly critical of this so-called 1812 policy. However, not only Karl XIV Johan but also Oskar I, at least during the first years of his reign, clung to it. Even as late as the armistice and peace negotiations of 1848–50, at the time of the Slesvig-Holstein War, Oskar I had taken the side of Tsar Nicholas I, mainly to offset radical German nationalism.

Oskar I's personal sympathies, however, were with those who opposed the accepted policy, and secretly he and his private collaborators, the so-called Royal Camarilla, were working for a reversal of foreign policy to liberate it from the conservative pro-Russian line adopted by his father in 1812. This only became possible when the Great Powers' conflict over Turkey and the control of the Bosphorus in 1853 led to the Crimean War between the Western Powers and Russia.

In this situation Oskar I, partly as an expression of his own pan-Scandinavian policies, opened negotiations with Denmark for a joint declaration of neutrality. Denmark's and Sweden-Norway's identically worded declarations of neutrality in December 1853 were, however, notably friendly toward the West. Scandinavian ports were to remain open, with only minor exceptions, to all foreign warships and merchant vessels. At the

'Agitation', painting by Hildur Hult-Wåhlin, 1899. In the later decades of the nineteenth century Swedish employers did everything they could to prevent the spread of socialist ideas. But agitators, devoted to the cause, appeared in workplaces. In the 1870s unions began to be formed to wrest better conditions from employers. The first nationwide trade union was formed in 1886, and in 1898 the nationwide Trade Union Confederation (LO). – Folkets Hus Stockholm. Photo: Lars Centerstam.

On Aug 15, 1854, an Anglo-French fleet bombarded the Russian fortress of Bomarsund in the Åland islands, which capitulated the next day, its 2,000-man garrison being taken prisoner. The fortress itself was afterwards blown up. To Oskar I's intense disappointment, however, the Allies limited their Baltic operations and concentrated instead on the Crimea. – The Royal Library, Stockholm.

same time Oskar I secretly gave the British government information as to which harbours would best serve as bases for the Royal Navy in the Baltic.

His disappointment was therefore intense when, in the summer of 1854, the Western Powers, instead of launching their attack from bases in Swedish harbours in the Baltic, made the Crimean fortress of Sebastopol their main target. He remarked bitterly that instead of 'seizing the giant by the throat' – viz. St. Petersburg – they had only stamped on his 'little toe'.

By intense propaganda in British and French newspapers and promises of Swedish support Oskar I tried to get the Western

100

Powers to change their strategy. His efforts led to the November treaties of 1855, which meant a definitive breach with Russia and the pro-Russian line in Swedish foreign policy.

The Treaty of Paris, however, signed soon afterwards, partly as a consequence of the November treaties and the implied threat of Sweden joining in the war on the side of the Western Powers, also put paid to any hopes Swedes had of at last recovering Finland, or at least the Åland islands. None of Oskar I's hopes of great achievements abroad had come to anything. All they amounted to was the Åland Convention, which demilitarized the islands and forbade Russia to build fortresses on them.

In the 1840s and 1850s many people, especially students and liberal circles in Denmark and Sweden, had been in favour of the idea of a Scandinavian Union. When Karl XV, upon his father falling ill in 1857, took over the government, Scandinavianism was at its peak. University students were forever holding meetings, making speeches and toasting the countries' common interests. Karl XV was also enthusiastic, and the union of the two countries became the great goal of his foreign policy.

In 1859 he succeeded to the throne and expressed his feelings of solidarity with Denmark, and when Germany threatened the south Danish frontier he, at a meeting at Skodsborg in 1863, promised his Danish colleague Frederik VII Swedish military support to defend the Ejder line, i.e. the southern border of Sleavig. But when in February 1864 war broke out between Denmark and Prussia, the Swedish government reneged on the king's promises and Denmark was left to her fate.

Everyone realized what a defeat this was for the king, and it meant the end of Scandinavianism as the guiding principle of Swedish foreign policy.

Prussia's defeat of Austria in 1866 and of France in 1870–71, followed in the latter year by the union of all Germany under the Kaiser, changed the whole balance of power in Europe. During the Franco-Prussian war Sweden had been officially neutral, but both Karl XV's and most Swedes' sympathies had been with France. The king's openly francophile feelings and his rash statements in letters that fell into German hands gave rise to sharp diplomatic controversies with Bismarck.

Oskar II, who succeeded his brother at the latter's death in 1872, saw things rather differently. He both admired and sympathized with Bismarck's new Germany. So his accession marked a change of orientation in foreign policy.

Connections with Germany were also becoming ever livelier. Swedish industry bought German products, German books were being read at Swedish universities, and Swedish officers and officials were emulating their German counterparts. Even during the Franco-Prussian war there had been champions of a more pro-German policy, and during the 1870s and 1880s most of the leading national newspapers came to support it.

Such being the situation, Oskar II initiated a change. His aim for Swedish foreign policy, in 1885, was 'a Germanic, Scandinavian, Italian alliance to be joined by Britain, with peace as its goal and facing both east and west'.

At the turn of the new century and during its first years the threat of a russified Finland under Bobrikov, its Russian governor-general, lent further stimulus to these pro-German policies. The Russian threat seemed all too real, and together with ever worsening conflicts with Norway made it natural for Sweden to side with Germany.

At the same time, however, strong elements in the swiftly growing workers' movement and in the Liberal Party demanded a rejection of the ever more blatant German imperialism. Thus the conditions for the neutrality which has characterized Sweden throughout the twentieth century began to take shape.

The explorer Adolf Erik
Nordenskiöld on the ice
of the Northeast Passage
in the winter of 1878–79,
painting by Georg von
Rosen, 1886. In the
background, the ice-
bound 'Vega'. It was the
first Arctic circumnaviga-
tion of Asia, an exploit
which unleashed immense
enthusiasm. Other
Swedish voyages of
discovery included S.A.
Andrée's unsuccessful
attempt to reach the
North Pole in his balloon
'The Eagle' in 1897 – its
relics were only found on
White Island in 1930.
Even more celebrated was
Sven Hedin, who explored
the interior of Asia. In the
first decades of the
twentieth century Erland
Nordenskiöld made
notable and valuable
explorations of South
America, and the geologist
and archeologist J.G.
Andersson did the same in
China. – The National Art
Museums, Stockholm.

103

# The Swedish-Norwegian Union, 1814–1905

The Swedish-Norwegian Union had been the fruit of several compromises. In the documents it was based on – the Treaty of Kiel, the Convention of Moss and the election of Karl XIII as King of Norway in November 1814 – these compromises had only been reached through formulas either party could interpret in its own way. Many fundamental clauses were so ambiguously formulated that from the outset they had in fact been quite differently understood. The Union wore quite a different aspect in Sweden from what it did in Norway.

Swedes thought of it as compensation for the loss of Finland. Norway was to be incorporated in a common realm, as Finland had been. But Norwegians saw the Union as a first step toward the independence the nation had been ever more loudly clamouring for in the years immediately preceding its imposition: a demand embodied in the Eidsvoll Constitution and the election of a king of their own on May 17, 1814. If they had accepted the Union under force majeure, it had been on condition that the King of Sweden accepted the Eidsvoll Constitution and undertook to respect Norway's autonomous status within the Union.

This attitude, prominent even in 1814, would never really change as long as the Union lasted.

When the Swedes, aiming to merge the two countries, tried in various ways to strengthen ties between them, their attempts were always stubbornly resisted. The Norwegians firmly rejected anything that might infringe their domestic autonomy, guaranteed by the Union treaties.

Since only a common crown held the two countries together, any attempt to strengthen its powers also tightened the bonds with Sweden. All conflicts in the Norway of the 1820s hinged on the question of the king's status and authority.

Under the Eidsvoll Constitution the Storting (the Norwegian Parliament) enjoyed greater powers than any other Parliament except in Britain and the USA. It could propose and implement new legislation even in the teeth of the royal veto. Thus in 1821, much against Karl XIV Johan's wishes, it abolished aristocracy in Norway, sticking to its guns even when the king tried to impose an absolute veto by intimidating the Storting with a display of military force. So unanimous was the resistance, the king had to yield; and thereafter the Storting's authority became the Norwegians' bulwark against any attempts by the monarch – i.e., the King of Sweden – to fuse his two realms into a single state.

The next epoch in the Union's history, from the mid-1830s to 1860, is marked by efforts to replace the ambiguous 1814 regulations by a new Union treaty in which the two countries' mutual relations and the functions of their common organs would be clearly defined. In 1844, after lengthy negotiations, such a bill was in fact presented, but rejected by the Norwegians, and in the end (1862), after endless and fruitless discussions, dropped. It had anyway been overshadowed by the first major Union conflict, namely the struggle over the governorship-general in 1859–60.

From the outset it had been taken for granted that the monarch should normally reside in Sweden, and the autumn 1814 modifications to the Eidsvoll Constitution stipulated that he was to be represented by a resident governor-general. This stipulation, immutable on the Swedish side but regarded in Norway as one of the most tangible signs of the country's subordinate status, the Norwegians repeatedly and emphatically demanded should be rescinded. In 1854 the Storting even unilaterally tried to alter this obnoxious clause of the Constitution, but its decision was vetoed by the king.

By then, however, the question had lost all real content – since 1829 the post had either been occupied by Norwegians, or even for long periods not been occupied at all. Upon its again falling vacant, in 1855, Oskar I omitted to appoint a new governor; but instead, in the following year, appointed the crown prince – the future Karl XV – viceroy. A measure received with great satisfaction in Norway.

Karl threw himself heart and soul into his viceregal functions,

J.A. Gripenstedt became consultant Councillor of State in 1848 and remained in government until 1866. As finance minister between 1856 and 1866 he did much to implement that period's numerous Liberal reforms. He also gained great influence over foreign policy by opposing Karl XV's plans to abolish the Norwegian governorship (1859) and support Denmark against Prussia (1863). – The Royal Library, Stockholm.

with a view to strengthening the Union, and even promised the Norwegians that he, at his accession, would abolish the governorship altogether, again with a view to creating conditions for a more durable solution.

Counting on this promise the Storting, at Karl XV's accession in 1859, again tried to abolish the governorship. But upon Karl XV approving its decision in the Norwegian Council of State, the Swedish Parliament and government, under the forceful finance minister, J.A. Gripenstedt, refused their consent. As Gripenstedt saw it, any such decision concerned the Union, and thus could not be unilateral and would have to be brought up before a joint Council of both countries. Upon the Norwegians refusing, and Gripenstedt's ministry, with strong parliamentary support, threatening to resign, Karl XV was obliged to yield and therefore withheld his approval of the Storting's decision.

From the Swedish point of view this was a victory for the ministry, with parliamentary support, over the crown. Indeed the whole governorship issue can be seen as the beginning of the long tug of war between them that would be the hallmark of Swedish political history during the later nineteenth century and up to 1914.

For Karl XV personally the outcome had been a grievous

defeat. His royal word had proved empty. His reign had been stricken at the root.

The dispute had also revealed the depth of the gulf between Swedes and Norwegians – a gulf which Karl XV, as viceroy, had already become aware of. Every attempt made during his reign (1859–72) to modify the Union's basic clauses would come to nothing, and so did his policy of strengthening the ties between the two countries. Not until shortly after his death would the governorship finally be abolished (1873), without any protest in Sweden.

Union conflicts would also infest the reign of Oskar II (1872–1907). Characteristic of its first phase would be Oskar II's obstinate attempts to assert his authority in Norway. The second phase would be marked by Norwegian determination to have their own minister for foreign affairs, and, more especially, their own consular system.

Shortly after Oskar II's accession in 1872 the Norwegian demand for full parliamentary government took expression in an Act permitting members of the Council of State to take part in the Storting's sessions, thus de facto turning them into its own representatives rather than the crown's. This Oskar II refused to sanction. Even when the Storting had passed the same bill three times – in 1874, 1877 and 1880 – he refused to promulgate it, declaring it to be a modification of the Constitution, under which the royal veto, as he saw it – and as was generally accepted in Sweden – was absolute, not merely suspensive.

Upon the Norwegian prime minister being impeached for countersigning the Act, the high court sided with the Storting and in 1884 disqualified the Conservative cabinet; whereupon Oskar II had to appoint a Liberal one, acceptable to the Storting. Norwegian parliamentary government had won a decisive victory.

But immediately fresh problems arose.

Even if Norway, in 1884, gained complete domestic autonomy, she was represented abroad by the Swedish-Norwegian king and his officials in the Swedish foreign office. It was the last

107

obstacle to complete Norwegian equality, and from now on the Union issue would hinge on the question of Norwegian representation abroad.

In 1885 the Swedish Parliament had increased its control of foreign affairs. This reform, though democratic in itself, meant that Norwegian foreign policy, implemented by the king through his Swedish foreign minister, would be even more subordinated to the Swedish authorities. An insistent demand was therefore raised for a Norwegian foreign office, under its own minister for foreign affairs. In 1891 it was on this platform the Norwegian Liberal (*venstre*) party won a resounding victory at the polls.

But though Oskar II had to accept a Liberal government, it side-stepped the question of a foreign minister in favour of the more limited demand for a consular system. This too Oskar II, when the Storting tried to implement it unilaterally, under strong Swedish pressure absolutely rejected. In the upshot both the Norwegian government and Storting were forced by threats of military action to negotiate a revision of the Union as a whole.

By this time the entire issue, despite Swedish concessions, had become so inflamed that no compromise was any longer possible. In 1898, after the negotiations had broken down and the Norwegians, flouting the royal veto, had removed the union quartering from their merchant ensign, an attempt was made to solve the more limited consular problem instead. These negotiations, too, proving sterile, the Norwegians took the matter into their own hands.

In May 1905 a bill was presented to and passed by the Storting to set up a Norwegian consular system. Upon Oskar II vetoing the reform, the Norwegian coalition government formed expressly to force the matter through resigned. Since the king could not form a new Norwegian cabinet, the Storting, on June 7, 1905, formally declared 'that the union with Sweden under one king is dissolved, the king having ceased to function as King of Norway'.

And that, in reality, was the end of the Union. The Swedish

Parliament, however, refused to accept the Storting's unilateral and, as it saw it, unconstitutional decision, demanded that the dissolution be legally negotiated and stipulated certain Swedish conditions for agreeing to it, among them the abandonment and demolition of fortresses erected in Norway along the Swedish frontier. At a conference held in Karlstad, Sweden, in September 1905 – after negotiations which at times had been dramatic and during which both countries had mobilized – the Union was dissolved by mutual agreement; which also put an end to it *de jure*.

Photo from 1888 of ore train on the railway between Luleå and Gällivare. Finished that year, its construction greatly advanced the exploitation of the rich North Swedish iron ore deposits. In 1898–1903 the railway system was extended to the Swedish-Norwegian frontier at Riksgränsen and down to the Norwegian ocean port of Narvik, which greatly expanded Swedish iron ore exports. In the Second World War Swedish iron ore exports via the ice-free port of Narvik were one of the reasons for Germany's attack on Norway on April 9, 1940.

# The Twentieth Century

## Parliamentary Democracy

Alongside the Union question, and well before its solution, the demand for universal equal suffrage had become the main issue in Swedish politics. The introduction of conscription in 1901 had lent it added strength under the rallying cry of 'one man, one rifle, one vote'.

The coalition cabinet, formed by the Conservative Christian Lundeberg to resolve the Union issue, had had to resign, and in the autumn of 1905 the Liberal leader Karl Staaff took over,

The franchise demonstrations of May 1902, seen through the satirical eyes of Arthur Sjögren, in his cartoon for the comic paper *Karbasen* (The Cane). 'Now he demands his rights, the working-class giant, who has so long and patiently borne his slave-yoke.'

Karl Staaff, leader of the Liberal Party, was prime minister 1905–1906, when the First Chamber's opposition to his proposals for a solution to the franchise issue forced him to resign. After the Liberals' massive victory at the polls in 1911 he formed a second cabinet, which resigned in Feb 1914 in protest against Gustaf V's so-called courtyard speech to the Farmers' Rally, in which he ignored his cabinet's views on the defence issue. Staaf's persistent demands for parliamentary government and democracy exerted a strong influence on Liberal politics. – The Royal Library, Stockholm.

above all with a view to resolving the franchise question. The 1906 bill proposed that all Swedish men should be equally entitled to elect the Second Chamber, in single-member constituencies. Upon the First Chamber, fearing this would produce a compact left-wing majority in the Second, throwing the bill out, the Staaff government too resigned and in 1906 was replaced by a Conservative government under Arvid Lindman. Its Franchise Act, passed in 1907 after lengthy negotiations and many compromises and ratified in 1909, introduced universal male suffrage for the Second Chamber, a reduced quota of votes related to income and fortunes in local government elections, and proportional elections for both Chambers.

The 1911 elections were the first under the new Act and a victory for the Liberals, whose position in the Second Chamber was now strong. In the First Chamber, however, the right-wing parties retained their majority. Staaff formed his second Liberal government. Even if King Gustaf V (1907–50) refused to acknowledge it and continued to regard ministers as representing himself, not Parliament, the election results had been a first triumph for parliamentary government.

113

In the Olympic Games held in Stockholm in 1912, 3,889 sportsmen participated, from 28 nations. The games drew 327,000 spectators and were an immense success for Sweden, which, in hard competition with USA, won more medals than any other country. – Poster, designed by Olle Hjortzberg. The Royal Library, Stockholm.

OLYMPISKA SPELEN
STOCKHOLM 1912
29 JUNI – 22 JULI

From 1911 onwards defence became the crucial issue. The threat of a war between the Triple Alliance and the Entente Cordiale was all too real. When Staaff had formed his Liberal cabinet, Gustaf V specifically minuted his support for a stronger defence; but Staaff, who had won the 1911 elections partly on a platform of disarmament and economy in military expenditure, despite the imminent threat of war in 1913 and 1914, refused to present a defence bill that would increase the military appropriations and prolong the 240-day conscription period.

Gustaf V, on the other hand, demanded an immediate decision to strengthen the country's defence, and the so-called Farmers' Rally was organized to support his policy. On February 6, 1914, more than 30,000 farmers marched up to the Palace

114

in Stockholm from all over the country, demanding an instant solution to the defence question and declaring their willingness to make any sacrifices the experts might require in the way of a longer conscription period and higher taxes. Addressing them from a balcony in the palace courtyard, Gustaf V openly told the farmers he did not share the prime minister's views on defence, which 'should be treated as a whole and decided now, without delay and in a single context' – thus explicitly declaring himself opposed to his cabinet's policy.

Gustaf V's attempt to force through his wishes unconstitutionally, regardless of the Second Chamber majority and by extra-parliamentary means, went far beyond the defence issue, as such. Who really ruled Sweden? King or Parliament? The question brought the struggle for parliamentary government to a head. Staaff tried to oblige the king to retract his promises by demanding that he publicly declare his speech not to have been an act of state, inasmuch as it had not been approved in advance by the cabinet. This Gustaf V refused to do, declaring 'I will not deprive myself of the right to speak freely to the Swedish people'.

A constitutional crisis followed. Only after protracted negotiations could Gustaf V prevail on a conservative-minded senior servant, Hjalmar Hammarskjold (father of the future UN Secretary-General Dag Hammarskjöld) to take over. The Hammarskjöld cabinet, for lack of parliamentary support or justification, was wholly monarchical. And indeed its first measure was to dissolve the Second Chamber and call an election.

The election results were dramatic. For the first time the Social Democrats became the largest party in the Second Chamber – a position they have held ever since.

Since Hammarskjöld's government could not obtain a majority for the royal policies, these could easily have ended in catastrophe both for Gustaf V and his dynasty. Abdication and a republic were being called for. In the upshot, however, the king was saved by the very issue with which he had precipitated the crisis. As it turned out, he had assessed the European situation more shrewdly than either Karl Staaff or the Social-Democrat

115

leader Hjalmar Branting had done. In June 1914 the shot was fired in Sarajevo.

The outbreak of war on August 1 led to mobilization, an end to political strife, and unanimity on defence. Neither Gustaf V nor Hammarskjöld's cabinet were ever called to account for the Farmers' Rally and the 'courtyard speech'.

Sweden declared herself neutral, and Hammarskjöld's government saw to it that she adhered strictly to the Hague Convention, which prescribes a neutral state's complete impartiality toward the warring parties. By the same token Sweden also asserted her right to trade with both. Upon the Allies' blockade of Germany becoming one of their most effective weapons, Sweden's formal neutrality turned almost wholly to Germany's advantage. This led to the Allies tightening their control of Swedish transoceanic shipping, and in the end blocking it altogether. However, this did not so much interrupt Sweden's exports to Germany as cripple her own incoming supplies. By 1916 the food shortage had become acute, and most goods had to be rationed. The unlimited submarine warfare, aggravated by USA's entry into the war in 1917, were strangling all imports from America. Food riots broke out in Stockholm and Gothenburg, and calls for Hammarskjöld's resignation became ever louder. The Conservative government which followed his resignation in the spring of 1917 opened negotiations with the Allies, resulting in an agreement that reopened imports from the West.

The war years saw a growing demand for parliamentary democracy. Upon the left-wing parties – Liberals and Social Democrats – winning a big majority in the Second Chamber in September 1917, the king could no longer refuse to sanction a left-wing government. Headed by the Liberal Nils Edén, it included – for the first time – four Social-Democrat ministers. Parliamentary government had made its definitive breakthrough.

Germany's defeat in 1918 unleashed demands for a more democratic order of things. In 1918–21 the Constitution was

116

revised, with the support of the government and of leading industrialists. Chief among its innovations were votes for women and universal franchise also in local government elections, which meant that the First Chamber, too, became more democratic. Sweden was now in all respects a democracy.

## Sweden's Second Great Age

The decades prior to the First World War had seen many new industries come into being. Many of them, particularly in engineering, were based on such Swedish inventions as Alfred Nobel's invention of dynamite, Gustaf de Laval's cream separator and steam turbine, Gustaf Dalén's Aga automatic lighthouse,

The three Scandinavian monarchs, Kristian X of Denmark, Gustaf V of Sweden and Håkon VII of Norway, at their meeting in Malmö, December 1914. The meeting, in which the three countries' foreign ministers took part, was a demonstration of Scandinavian unity and determination to remain neutral during the First World War. – TV Archives, SVT.

117

Sven Wingquist's self-regulating ball bearings, L.M. Ericsson's table telephone, Jonas Wenström's three-phase system for alternating current, and Baltzar von Platen's absorption-method refrigerator. These inventions had led to the founding and development of such firms as Bofors (armaments), Separator (today's Alfa Laval), Aga (gas, tooling steel), SKF (ball bearings) L.M. Ericsson (telecommunication systems), ASEA (electrical engineering, renamed ABB since its fusion with Brown Boveri in 1988) and Electrolux (domestic electric equipment, etc.). The pulp industry's rapid development had also been due to technological progress.

The 1920s, the decade when Swedish industry made its great breakthrough, have rightly been called 'Sweden's Second Great Age'. All the above enterprises went international. Swedish shipyards became a major industry; and for a while Sweden enjoyed a virtually world-wide monopoly of match production. From having been a deeply indebted country with heavy capital imports, she transformed herself in the 1920s into one whose industries were founding world-wide subsidiaries. All this radically changed her economy.

One reason for Sweden's inter-war expansion was that wages did not rise as fast as output. There was an increase in the numbers of industrial workers and of the urban population. Prior to the First World War over half of all Swedes had lived in the countryside. After the Second World War more than three-quarters were living in urbanized areas, a development accelerated by the mechanization of agriculture. Here an important step was the electrification of the countryside in the 1920s.

Such swift technological and economic developments led to great social changes. In 1914 the old-age pension had been introduced, however inadequate its extent; and in 1920 the workers' movement had forced through its long-standing demand for an 8-hour working day. Trade union power grew, and wages began rising faster than prices. Not that class differences in the inter-war period were not still very great; and overall living standards were only very slowly improving. One factor, here,

118

Alfred Nobel, chemist, 1833–96, created an international industrial concern on the basis of his construction of an efficient detonator and his invention of dynamite. In his will he stipulated that the major part of his very big fortune should be converted into a fund and invested, the income to be 'distributed annually in the form of prizes to those who during the preceding year have conferred the greatest benefit on mankind' in a number of fields. Except during the two World Wars Nobel Prizes have been presented annually since 1901. – The Royal Library, Stockholm.

was that Sweden, like other West European countries, was badly hit by the economic crisis of the early 1930s. Unemployment rose sharply, and numerous industrial conflicts aggravated the situation. Only at the decade's end did the economic situation become stabler, reopening the path to greater prosperity.

## From Scale-Tipping to Majority Governments

Up to 1920 Liberals and Social Democrats had been held together by their common demand for parliamentary government. But no sooner was it satisfied by the 1918–21 constitutional reforms than other questions came to the fore.

The Social Democratic movement, dominated at that time by a group of radical socialists, was calling for nationalization of the country's natural assets and industries. The Liberals stood for private property and free enterprise. Now the political watershed no longer ran between right-wing and left-wing parties, but between socialist and non-socialist parties – a cleavage which remains and is still politically crucial.

The breach between Social Democrats and Liberals having cost the Edén government its parliamentary majority, it had to

119

resign in March 1920. At the same time the political regrouping destroyed the possibility of a stable majority for the new government, since the Liberal and Conservative parties still held widely different views on many questions. In this situation Sweden got her first purely Social Democratic government, with Hjalmar Branting as prime minister.

The war years had also seen the formation of a farmers' party. Along with the Conservatives, the Liberals and the Social Democrats, the Agrarian Party would become one of Sweden's four main political parties.

Sole common denominator of the non-socialist parties was their opposition to the Social Democratic government's economic policy. Their differences in other matters remained sharp, sometimes irreconcilable. Having no basis for collaboration, they could not form a majority government; and after Hjalmar Branting's Social Democratic government's defeat at the polls in October 1920, one minority government followed another. This left power essentially with Parliament, where Conservative, Liberal and Social-Democratic minority governments had to take turn and turn about by leaning on temporary constellations and taking each issue by itself.

The first years of the 1920s bore the imprint of the profound post-war economic crisis, and from 1921 to 1923 the Swedish labour market was disturbed by widespread unemployment and rising monetary values. In 1925, the Social Democrats introduced a new defence system, reduced the conscription period, and abolished many regiments. Another major issue, educational reform, was resolved by the 1927 Liberal government's Education Act. Labour market conditions were regulated by laws – passed with Conservative support in 1928 – that introduced collective bargaining and set up a labour court to mediate in disputes.

Like other countries, Sweden was stricken from 1930 onwards by the world-wide economic crisis that had broken out in the USA in the autumn of 1929. Sharply rising unemployment and falling wages unleashed conflicts in the labour market.

120

The walrus moustached Social-Democratic leader Hjalmar Branting in a peace demonstration in Stockholm in the summer of 1924. Organized to mark the tenth anniversary of the outbreak of the First World War, it also stressed Sweden's involvement in the collective security policy which later that year led to the League of Nation's so-called Geneva Protocol. Branting, shortly to become prime minister for the third time, had been one of its chief protagonists. His efforts for world peace and international collaboration made him the best known of all Sweden's prime ministers – with the possible later exception of Olof Palme. – Pressens Bild.

These culminated in 1931 in a demonstration in the Ådalen Valley, in northern Sweden, where the military opened fire on the crowd, killing five people. Shortly afterwards, in the spring of 1932, tensions were further aggravated by the suicide of the country's biggest financier, the 'Swedish Match King' Ivar Kreuger. Unemployment reached new record levels.

121

The September 1932 elections being a great victory for the Social Democrats, the Liberal government was followed by a Social Democratic cabinet under Per Albin Hansson. Despite their victory at the polls – won by promising to actively combat unemployment along New Deal lines and a programme based on theories of an active trade-cycle policy, one of whose authors was the British economist J.M. Keynes – the Social Democrats lacked a parliamentary majority. Since the policy's cornerstone was the provision of major public works, paid for with market wages in lieu of the dole, it came in for severe criticism from the non-socialist parties, anxious to cut back on government spending.

To implement its policy the Social Democratic government therefore turned to the Agrarian Party, which agreed to support it in exchange for agricultural subsidies. After the 1936 elections the two parties' collaboration became manifest in a coalition government headed by Per Albin Hansson, which enjoyed a parliamentary majority.

Meanwhile times had improved, and the late 1930s saw falling unemployment. Finally, in December 1938 an agreement was reached between the two main parties on the labour market, the Employers' Confederation and the Trade Union Confederation. Under this arrangement, known as the Saltsjöbaden Agreement after the place where it was concluded, the forms to be taken by negotiations, agreements and any future conflicts were regulated as binding upon the employers' and employees' associations. The outcome was a collaboration which greatly reduced conflicts on the labour market and contributed to Sweden's swift economic growth during the decades immediately following the Second World War.

Politically, however, the decade had been a time of preparation. Parliamentary committees had been appointed and bills drawn up to realize what the Social Democrats called *folkhemmet* (the 'people's home'), i.e. the welfare state. Their fiscal policy was to increase taxes for the higher income brackets, move toward a redistribution of incomes and fortunes, introduce a general pension system based on the individual's working life, improve medical and social care, renew the country's housing and reform the educational system, with 9-year obligatory schooling for all. Ideologically this programme implied a soft-pedalling of socialist demands. Nor would the welfare state nationalize the means of production. On the other hand it would automatically increase the state's responsibilities and economic influence.

Only a small part of the Social Democratic programme could be implemented during the 1930s. In 1939 the outbreak of the Second World War brought a political truce, all the country's resources being mobilized to defend Swedish neutrality. Government plans for major social and economic reforms had to be postponed.

## Neutrality and Solidarity

The two prime factors bearing on inter-war Swedish foreign policy had been the Soviet Union's attempt to exert greater influence in the Baltic, and the threat from Germany.

Throughout the 1920s, Russia and Germany, the losers in the First World War, had both been very weak. Sweden, which had come to dominate the Baltic, seemed to have no security problems. So the 1925 Defence Act radically cut her armed forces.

Sweden had also joined the League of Nations, founded in 1920. Since membership involved an undertaking to resist an aggressor in the event of the Security Council imposing sanctions, the question arose whether this was compatible with Sweden's traditional neutrality. The problem was solved by reserving her position on this point – a reservation, however, never accepted by the Great Powers. Nor, luckily, would it ever be put to the test during the inter-war years.

Finland's declaration of independence on December 6, 1917, was enthusiastically received in Sweden. When, shortly afterwards, a civil war broke out between those Finns who wanted

123

a socialist revolution and the 'whites' who resisted it, Swedish public opinion was strongly on the side of the whites, and Conservatives even called for active intervention. This being firmly opposed by the left-wing government, Swedish support for the whites, who comprised most of Finland's Swedish-speaking population, went no further than a volunteer corps.

The civil war over, the question of the Åland islands arose. In a referendum, 95 per cent of the islands' – wholly Swedish-speaking – population had declared for reunion with Sweden. When Finland objected, the question was submitted to the League of Nations, where it was decided that Åland should form a part of Finland, in return for Finnish guarantees of the population's political autonomy and an undertaking not to fortify the islands or use them for military bases. For a while the League's decision, resented in Sweden, dampened the two countries' otherwise cordial relations.

Throughout the 1920s and the first half of the 1930s Sweden relied on the League to guarantee her security, but after Hitler had seized power in 1933 and Germany had left the League, her position seemed less secure. After the Abyssinian war of 1935–36 had demonstrated the League's impotence, and Hitler, in March 1936, had defied the Treaty of Versailles by remilitariz-ing the Rhineland, Sweden, together with six other small neutral states, in July 1936 declared herself no longer bound by the League's statutes on sanctions. She had reverted to simple neutrality.

Such isolated neutrality hardly being able to guarantee her security in a time of ever acuter Great Power conflicts, Sweden turned instead to her Nordic neighbours. Both Denmark and Norway rejected, however, the proposals put forward in April 1938 by the Swedish foreign minister Rickard Sandler. Only Finland remained, and talks were continued, notably for defend-ing Åland; but in May 1939 this project, comprised in the so-called Stockholm Plan, was vetoed by the Soviet Union. At the same time Sweden underlined her neutrality by rejecting Hitler's proposal for a non-aggression pact.

124

Per Albin Hansson holding a speech. He succeeded Hjalmar Branting, the Social Democratic Party's first leader, after his death in 1925. In 1928 elected chairman, he was prime minister from 1932 until his death in 1946 and exerted an authoritative sway over government. During the Second World War, as leader of the coalition, he became almost universally accepted as a wise father figure.
– Pressens Bild.

## The Second World War

At the outbreak of war in September 1939 all the Nordic countries declared themselves neutral. The Soviet ultimatum to Finland, demanding territorial concessions in the east and the right to establish a naval base on Hangö at the mouth of the Gulf of Finland, precipitated, in November 1939, an attack on the smaller country, and placed a severe strain on Swedish policy. The discussions, which had already begun, on a common defence and the idea of Nordic solidarity may well have been a factor in the Finns' rejection of the Soviet demands. However, when bombs began falling on Helsinki on November 30, 1939, Sweden was not prepared to intervene; and Sandler, who had been the author of the idea of a collaboration and was in favour of Swedish intervention, had to resign.

In December 1939 national unanimity found expression in a coalition government. It comprised the four major democratic parties, with Per Albin Hansson as prime minister. Though Sweden declared herself 'non-combatant' in the war between the Soviet Union and Finland, public opinion was completely pro-Finnish and under the slogan 'Finland's cause is ours' it insisted that the Finns be given all possible help short of actual military intervention. Again a volunteer corps was organized. More important, however, was the massive support in materiel, which included weapons and ammunition, aircraft and vehicles. On the other hand, for fear of becoming involved in the Great Power conflict, Sweden turned down an Allied request for troops to be allowed to cross Swedish territory. When the Finns, despite their stiff and by no means unsuccessful resistance, were forced to retreat, Sweden mediated a peace offer that in March 1940 led to the Treaty of Moscow.

The Finnish Winter War was followed on April 9, 1940, by the German attack on Denmark and Norway. No plans for invading Sweden ever seem to have existed. What the Germans did demand was the right to transit troops and materiel across Swedish territory. Throughout April and May, as long as the fighting was going on in Norway, Sweden again refused, only allowing transits of Red Cross supplies; but when the fighting ended and France had fallen she felt she had no option but to allow German 'leave troops' and all kinds of materiel to be transported in Swedish rolling stock to and from Norway. Faced with the possibility of a German ultimatum and the situation in that summer of 1940 being what it was, Sweden had only one course to follow.

In June 1941 Germany demanded a further concession in connection with her assault on the Soviet Union; this time for rail transit of a fully armed division – the so-called Engelbrecht Division – from Norway to Finland. Refusal was not out of the question; but the Swedish government decided to accede, partly seeing it as a way of helping Finland, now again at war with the Soviet Union.

126

The German occupation of Denmark and Norway had cut off Sweden's western trade, and this, together with the poor harvests of 1940 and 1941, caused a shortage of food and other important commodities. Rationing was introduced and would persist long after the war was over.

By separate negotiations with both sides, permission was, however, obtained for a limited number of Swedish ships to pass through the Allied blockade and the German Skagerack minefields – the so-called safe-conduct traffic. Meanwhile the Allies had chartered that part of the Swedish merchant marine which had been outside the German mine-fields on April 9, 1940.

Except for this safe-conduct traffic Swedish trade was now restricted to imports and exports with Germany and the German-occupied countries. Crucial, here, were her iron ore exports

Finnish refugee children arriving in Sweden during the Second World War. Besides sending a volunteer corps, Sweden supported Finland with voluntary donations, weapons, aircraft, ammunition and other war materiel. But most important of all perhaps, was the refuge given to Finnish children whose numbers by 1944 had added up to 36,000. – Pressens Bild.

to Germany and imports of coal from the same quarter. To the Allies Sweden was an important island of neutrality in a German-occupied Europe – particularly so for Danish and Norwegian refugees and the links with the resistance movements of these two countries.

When German victories were followed by defeats, Sweden began to revise her policies, and in July 1943, without her suffering any reprisals, the leave-traffic agreement was unilaterally rescinded.

Sweden's humanitarian efforts were considerable. Several exchanges of prisoners of war took place in Gothenburg. She also welcomed refugees, first mainly from the Baltic states, then also from Norway and Denmark. One important event, here, was the reception of some 7,500 Danish Jews who, threatened with deportation to Germany, fled to Sweden in September 1943. Even more extensive was the rescue, by Count Folke Bernadotte's 'white busses', of tens of thousands of concentration camp victims in the spring of 1945.

Count Folke Bernadotte and the British brigadier-general N.O. Lash, Glubb Pasha's right-hand man in the Arab Legion, at the Jerusalem negotiations of 1948. On May 21, 1948, the UN Security Council had appointed Folke Bernadotte mediator in the conflict which had just led to open war between Israel and the Arab states. After he had brought about an armistice, in June, he led intensive efforts to achieve a peaceful agreement. But on the eve of presenting his peace plan to the UN, on Sept 17, 1948, he was assassinated in Jerusalem by Jewish terrorists. – Pressens Bild.

## The Welfare State

As the war's end came in sight the Social Democrats, who ever since the 1940 elections had had an absolute majority in both Chambers of Parliament, began to look optimistically to the future. The war years having concentrated power in government hands, and with the state's influence on the economy and industry greater than ever, they envisaged few obstacles to carrying through their post-war programme of working-class reforms, worked out under the chairmanship of the finance minister, Ernst Wigforss. What had only been sketched out in the 1930s now seemed within close reach of realization.

In July 1945, shortly after the armistice, the coalition government resigned and was replaced by a Social Democratic cabinet, also under Per Albin Hansson, who remained prime minister until his death in 1946. His successor, Tage Erlander, would hold the post until 1969.

The 1945–51 period has rightly been regarded as the great Social Democratic 'harvest home'. Reform followed reform. In 1946, the old-age pension was raised to subsistence level and it was also decided to introduce a general sickness benefit scheme. In 1947, child allowances free of means test were introduced. A social housing policy enabled low-income families to move into modern apartments, while state loans and subsidies stimulated the building of new homes, particularly by the public sector. In 1948, a new Workers' Protection Act was passed and the annual holiday was lengthened from two to three weeks. In 1950, a 9-year comprehensive school was decided on. Already, in 1947, subsidies to universities and university colleges had been greatly increased, and plans were being worked out to expand research and higher education.

Most of these reforms were unanimous. In 1944 the Liberals who under Bertil Ohlin's leadership had become the main non-socialist party, had outlined their own social policy, largely identical with the Social Democrats'. Where the two parties' views differed was as to how these reforms should be financed. New taxes, presented by Ernst Wigforss and voted through in 1947, ran into stiff opposition. The main issues were the new, more steeply progressive income tax scales; a progressive capital tax; and an extra death duty, payable prior and in addition to the existing death duties, which were also increased. This last measure being seen as a move toward total socialization, it came in for particularly sharp criticism.

At the 1948 elections the Social Democats lost their absolute majority in the Second Chamber, but despite the big Liberal victory, the two socialist parties – Social Democrats and Communists – still had one jointly. Even so, the Social Democratic movement, impressed by the election results, dropped its post-war plans for nationalizing banks, insurance companies and certain sections of industry.

In 1951 the Korean War brought a sharp price rise and, at the same time as unemployment rose, the bills began to come in for all these major reforms. The state's finances were catastrophically affected by inflation and steeply rising expenditure. To strengthen his government Tage Erlander therefore formed a coalition with the Agrarians. Between 1951 and 1957 there was a pause in the work of reform, every effort at the same time being made to fully implement those already decided on.

Politically the 1950s were a period of political reaction. Though the 1956 elections lost the socialist block its majority in the Second Chamber, there was no change in the coalition government.

It was in this situation that the Social Democrats called for the introduction of a supplementary pension system (ATP).

The reform's background lay in the enormous gulf between white-collar and blue-collar pensions. Though the old-age pension had been raised in 1946, its real value had been undermined by inflation. But it was all a blue-collar worker got. A white-collar worker, on the other hand, normally received two-thirds of his final salary. This gap had been still further widened by rising wages and salaries, so that in the 1950s the old-age pension amounted to only one-tenth of the average wage of an industrial worker.

This pension issue would dominate domestic politics from 1957 to 1960. A referendum presented two proposals, plus a third line: on the one hand the Social Democrats' scheme for an obligatory supplementary pension, to be ongoingly financed by employers' dues; another, voluntary scheme was supported by the Agrarian Party; and a third scheme was for a voluntary system, under which pensions should be included in employer–union wage agreements and financed by premiums, in the normal way. This 'third' line was supported by the Conservatives and Liberals.

The referendum in October 1957 gave 46 per cent of the votes to the Social-Democrat line; 15 per cent to the second; and to the third 35 per cent. Only 4 per cent of the nation cast a blank ballot. This referendum success – 15 per cent as compared with

131

Laminated housing, Solna, outside Stockholm. The commonest type of apartment housing in Sweden since the Second World War its buildings do not stand in closed street blocks but are laid out in parallel lines or free-standing groups. During the 1960s the so-called Million Project created over 100,000 modern apartments annually, mainly in laminated suburban buildings. – The Museum of Architecture, Stockholm.

only 9.4 per cent at the polls – encouraged the Agrarian Party (now rebaptized the Centre Party) to withdraw from its coalition with the Social Democrats. Tage Erlander therefore formed a purely Social Democratic cabinet and presented a pension bill in line with his party's proposals. When the Second Chamber threw it out, he dissolved it.

At the extra elections of 1958 the Social Democrats gained 5 new seats, the Conservatives 3, and the Liberals lost no fewer than 20. The upshot was that in the Second Chamber the socialist and non-socialist block had 115 seats apiece, but the abstention of a working-class Liberal Party member at a renewed voting on the pension question enabled the Social Democrats to push through their ATP scheme. When the Conservatives proposed in the 1960 elections to abolish it, they were heavily defeated, thus restoring to the Social Democrats their dominant position, despite their lack of a majority and their dependence on the Communists.

Worsening trade conditions and rising unemployment had typified the first half of the 1950s. The second half saw stabler conditions. The 1960s being a period of sharply rising production and steady growth, further reforms became feasible. This situation was chiefly exploited to reinstate the real monetary value of earlier reforms and to develop child care, the health service and care of the elderly to the point where they could meet the demands being placed on them by the welfare state. Once again working hours were shortened. The annual holiday was extended to four weeks. The comprehensive school was introduced. The upper secondary school was reformed, and universities and university colleges were greatly expanded. Thus the 1960s became a second period of 'harvest home' for social reform.

## New Constitutional Laws

Up to 1970 Sweden's constitutional laws had been the Instrument of Government of 1809, the Parliament Act of 1866 (which occupies a position midway between constitutional and ordinary law) and the Act of Succession of 1810, together with the Freedom of Expression Act of 1812, replaced in its entirety after the Second World War by a new and more up to date one in 1949.

A clause in the 1809 Constitution had defined the Crown's functions with the words: 'the king alone rules the realm'. The only restriction on the royal prerogative was the king's duty to heed advice from a Council appointed by himself. Under Karl XIV Johan, and even under Oskar I, this system had corresponded to realities. But long before any change in the Constitution itself was proposed, democratic parliamentary developments had reduced it to a dead letter, and when the franchise for electing the First Chamber had become virtually identical with the rules for electing the Second, the division of Parliament into two Chambers, too, had lost most of its justification.

In the early 1950s it was therefore decided to work out a new constitution, and in 1954 a constitutional commission had been set up, which finished its work in 1963. After its findings had been widely debated and subjected to further commissions of enquiry, a bill was presented for a new Parliament Act, which was passed in 1970. It reduced Parliament to a single Chamber, with 350 – later changed to 349 – seats. It was to be reelected by proportional representation every third year, in 28 constituencies, and with a number of equalizing mandates to make it truly proportional.

The new Instrument of Government, adopted in 1974, came into effect in 1975, and it declares all public power to stem from the people, whose right and duty it is, by free and secret ballot, to elect Parliament, which alone legislates and levies taxes, and appoints a government responsible to Parliament. The king, though all his former political functions have been transferred to other organs, retains his status as head of state. Most importantly, it is now the speaker, not the monarch, who decides which party leader shall form a government and appoints him prime minister. It is the prime minister, no longer the king, who presides over cabinet meetings. Nor is the king any longer commander in chief of the armed forces, which come exclusively under the government. Today the king's duties are largely ceremonial.

At his death Gustaf VI Adolf (1950–73) was succeeded by Carl XVI Gustaf, the first king to reign – but not rule – under the new constitution. By a change in the succession rules in 1979 women now have the same hereditary right to the crown as men. Thus Princess Victoria, not her younger brother Prince Carl Philip, will be the present king's successor.

# Neutrality and International Involvement

When the 1948 Communist coup in Czechoslovakia and the Berlin Blockade had led to a sharpening of the international crisis, the Swedish and Danish governments made a joint proposal to open negotiations for a Scandinavian defence union. Sweden's point of view at these talks was that such a union should remain independent of the Great Powers. Norway's point of view, however, after her experiences in the Second World War, was that a union could only come into being in close collaboration with the West, and therefore she accepted instead an invitation to join the North Atlantic Treaty Organization

King Carl XVI Gustaf and Queen Silvia, and their three children: Crown Princess Victoria, b. 1977, Prince Carl Philip, b. 1979, and Princess Madeleine, b. 1982. In 1980 the rules for the succession were altered to admit the feminine line, which means that Princess Victoria, not her younger brother Carl Philip, will succeed to the throne. – Photo: Charles Hammarsten/Allers Photo Press.

(NATO), just then being formed. The Scandinavian talks collapsed and in this situation Denmark, too, joined NATO, while Sweden chose to remain outside.

Throughout the post-war period the guiding principle of Swedish foreign policy was 'non-participation in alliances in peacetime aiming at neutrality in the event of war'. Even so, Sweden has energetically involved herself in debates within the United Nations where she has done her best to help find solutions to other countries' conflicts. Her international status as a peacemaker was underlined by the appointment in 1953 of Dag Hammarskjöld as Secretary-General.

Within the UN framework – but also by actively supporting liberation movements – Sweden has helped the former colonies to free themselves and gain recognition as independent states. On several occasions she has also placed military units at the UN's disposal for tasks e.g. in the Congo and the Middle East, where Swedish UN troops have supervised armistices both in Cyprus and on the Israeli frontiers. By her humanitarian actions and – in proportion to her population of only 8.8 millions – her generous financial support to developing countries she has tried to reduce conflicts and preserve the peace.

But notwithstanding the neutrality policy there have been occasions when Swedish public opinion has very definitely taken sides. Such was the case, for instance, during the Vietnam War (1965–73) when she was so severely critical of United States policy that for a while the American ambassador was called home from Stockholm and there was a marked deterioration in the two countries' otherwise excellent relations. Sweden has also protested sharply against South African apartheid, economic relations being broken off and not resumed until the early 1990s. The coup d'état in Chile in 1973 made a shocking impression, and Sweden welcomed many political refugees both from there and other South American dictatorships.

Swedes also objected strongly to the Soviet occupation of Afghanistan in the 1980s – a reaction reinforced when in October 1981 a Soviet submarine, the U 137, ran aground in

136

A Swedish Catalina sea-rescue plane was shot down by Soviet fighter aircraft over the Baltic in the summer of 1952, its crew saving themselves in inflatable dinghies. The Catalina was searching for a military aircraft, equipped to trace radio signals, which had disappeared a few days before. Many years later it has transpired that the reconnaissance plane, too, had been shot down by a Soviet fighter, with the loss of its eight-man crew. The affair led to sharp protests to the Soviet Union, which maintained that the reconnaissance plane had infringed Soviet airspace

Gåsefjärden outside the Swedish naval base of Karlskrona, i.e. in a restricted zone. Throughout the 1980s Swedish-Soviet official relations, though never directly affected, were strained by this incident and by other Soviet submarines' violations of territorial waters and by Soviet fighter aircraft's violations of Swedish airspace over Gotland.

With the dissolution of the Soviet Union, Sweden, in 1991, recognized the three Baltic states, which she has thereafter supported with cash and credits, various material help and cultural contributions. In January 1992 Sweden also recognized the autonomous Russian, Ukrainian and White Russian republics.

Throughout the post-war period Swedish commercial policy has aimed at liberalizing and demolishing the various obstacles to free trade, mostly in close collaboration with Great Britain. In 1959 she was closely involved in setting up the European Free Trade Association (EFTA).

Even though plans for a Scandinavian defence union had come to nothing, Nordic collaboration in other respects had remained a leitmotif of post-war Swedish policy. One important step was the setting up of the Nordic Council in 1952. Among its achievements has been the abolition of passport controls between the Nordic countries, a common labour market, and close co-ordination of these countries' economic and social legislation. On the other hand efforts to set up a Nordic customs union within EFTA came to nought, its plans in 1968–70 for far-reaching economic co-operation ceasing to be feasible when Finland could not join. When Great Britain and Denmark joined the Common Market in 1972, the same question was discussed in Sweden; but such membership being found incompatible with Swedish neutrality, no concrete plans were made.

Germany's reunification and the dissolution of the Warsaw Pact has changed all this. In 1991, the Social Democratic government applied for membership in the European Community. Then in January 1995, after the decision had been confirmed in November 1994 by a referendum in which just over 52 per cent voted yes, Sweden became a member of the European Union (EU). On the other hand the population's lukewarm interest in and negative attitude toward EU was manifested in the September 1995 elections to the European Parliament, where only 41 per cent of the electorate participated, compared with over 86 per cent who had voted in the 1994 elections to the Swedish Parliament. What is more, half of the 22 EU representatives elected had been critical of Sweden becoming a member at all.

As a result of the negotiations about and Sweden's entry into the EU, there has been a change in the conditions for her traditional neutrality. During his period of premiership (1991–94)

138

Carl Bildt, for instance, declared it no longer to be a concept that correctly described the fundamental line in Swedish foreign policy. When Ingvar Carlsson became prime minister in 1994, however, he laid greater emphasis on Sweden's freedom from alliances, as did Göran Persson when entering on the same office in March 1996. Both Carlsson and Persson, while stressing the obligations implied by membership, have clearly emphasized that Sweden has at present no intention of involving herself in any military cooperation within EU. At the same time Sweden, in consort with NATO units, has participated in peace-keeping operations in what used to be Yugoslavia. In 1996 Swedish units, within the framework of Partnership for Peace (PFP), also took part in joint manoeuvres with NATO forces both in the Baltic and the North Sea.

Within the framework of the so-called Baltic Council – an informal collaborative organ founded in 1990 by the states around the Baltic – all heads of government from these – as they are today – eleven countries met on a Swedish initiative at Visby on 3-5 May 1996. Not only the German chancellor Helmut Kohl and the Russian prime minister Viktor Tjernomyrdin were present, but also Jacques Santer, president of the European Commission. The conference culminated in a manifestation for future peace and security in the Baltic region. Further confirmation of Sweden's leading role in collaborating with the other Baltic countries was provided in August 1996 at the meeting between the Swedish prime minister Göran Persson and US president Bill Clinton.

At the 1996–97 Intergovernmental Conference (IGC) Sweden urged that the three Baltic states Estonia, Latvia and Lithuania should be accepted as EU members at the earliest opportunity. During a visit to Riga in June 1996 Göran Persson also expressed Sweden's support for their application to join NATO. This in turn gave rise to a Swedish debate on Sweden's proposed membership, the government being firmly opposed.

At the turn of the new year 1996/97 Swedish foreign policy was dominated by the responsibility Sweden assumes and the lines she must take as a member of the UN Security Council as from 1 January 1997.

At the same time the question of a European Monetary Union was becoming crucial in internal discussions of foreign policy. Should Sweden, like the majority of EU countries, participate in the third phase in realizing such a union, implying as it must the introduction, from 1999 onwards, of a common currency and a central bank? The Riksdag is to decide on this in the autumn of 1997.

## Crises and New Governments

In 1969 Tage Erlander retired, after being prime minister since 1946. He was succeeded by Olof Palme, but there were no other changes in the Social Democratic government. At the 1970 elections, the first since the single Chamber reform, the Social Democrats lost the absolute majority they had enjoyed since 1968, but remained in power with the support of the Communists. At the next elections, in 1973, the left-wing parties lost some more seats, resulting in a hung Parliament, with 175 seats apiece for the socialist and non-socialist parties – a circumstance which led to the number of seats being reduced to 349, in order to avoid such a state of affairs for the future. Olof Palme's Social Democratic cabinet remained in power, though it had to find solutions in collaboration with the non-socialists, notably the Liberals.

The next elections, in 1976, gave the non-socialists a definite victory, 180 seats against 169 for the two socialist parties. This meant the end of 44 years of Social Democratic rule in Sweden. The new government consisted of a coalition of the Conservatives (renamed Moderates), the Liberals and the Centre, under the Centre leader Thorbjörn Fälldin.

The international crisis unleashed by the dramatic rise in oil prices in 1973 increased unemployment. Up to the early 1970s a combination of industrial expansion, which had been rapid during the 1950s and 1960s, together with swiftly rising production, had led to a sharp and steady rise in living standards. Since the mid-1970s this development fell off and in the late 1980s ceased altogether. At the same time Swedish politics had come to revolve around such new problems as the demand for employee participation in decision-making and democracy in work places, women's equality, the environment, and energy.

Here it was the question of nuclear energy which initially came into the foreground, and whether to extend the existing number of nuclear power stations. It was this latter issue which brought down the non-socialist coalition government. Thorbjörn Fälldin's and the Centre Party's platform at the 1976 elections, namely, had been a promise to halt the building of more nuclear power stations and then gradually dismantle those which already existed. Within the coalition government, however, the Liberals and Conservatives, who were in favour of more nuclear power, had forced Fälldin to make one concession after another. This led to his resignation in October 1978, his government being followed by a Liberal minority government under Ola Ullsten. When Ullsten could not solve the nuclear power question, all parties agreed in April 1979 to submit it to a referendum, to be held in March 1980.

Meanwhile other matters, economic problems and, more especially, high marginal taxation, came to the fore in the elections of September 1979. These were a victory for the Moderate Party, i.e. the former Conservatives, at the expense of the other non-socialist parties, while both socialist parties improved their position, albeit without gaining a majority. The Liberal government resigned and was replaced by a three-party cabinet under Thorbjörn Fälldin.

In the 1980 referendum on nuclear power, voters were given three choices. The outcome was that 58 per cent voted for expansion up to a maximum of twelve reactors, combined with an undertaking to gradually abolish them over a period of time to be decided by Parliament. In 1981 an Act was then passed that all reactors should be closed down by the year 2010 at the latest.

As a result of this decision the nuclear power question ceased to occupy the political foreground, and interest turned above all to the economic problems of inflation and the huge deficits both in the state finances and in the balance of payments.

These deficits had been due to global structural changes in industrial output and raw materials, which had been occurring since the early 1970s and which had led to a deep crisis, notably in Sweden's shipyard and textile industries, a crisis which in turn rubbed off onto iron and steel, whose structures had had to be rationalized. This caused unemployment to rise sharply in 1980–82. The economic problems, which mostly still remain, were further aggravated by a most unequal distribution of unemployment between branches, thus also between regions. Together with ever slower overall economic growth, society's expensive support for these industries precipitated a crisis which in the autumn of 1980 and spring of 1981 sharpened the conflicts between the three non-socialist parties then in power. These conflicts came to a head over the bill to lower marginal taxes these parties had promised the electorate. In May 1981 the Moderates withdrew, leaving the government to be reformed as a two-party alliance of Centre and Liberals, under Thorbjörn Fälldin.

The 1982 elections hinged on three issues: employment, the budget deficit, and the Social Democrats' proposal to set up an employee fund system. The Social Democrats won and Olof Palme formed a new government. The election results also showed how strongly polarized Swedish politics had become. The Moderates gained 13 seats, while Liberals and Centre together lost no fewer than 25.

Palme's new government immediately took drastic measures to improve the economic situation. Devaluating the krona by 16 per cent, it raised value-added tax by 2 per cent, at the same time putting pressure on the unions not to demand full compensation for the ensuant price rises. These measures, together with improvement in the international trade cycle in 1983 and 1984, reduced unemployment and somewhat improved Sweden's economic situation. After a few years it also became possible to reduce the budget deficit to a more acceptable level and, in the late 1980s, to get rid of it altogether.

Improved international trade conditions in the 1980s led to a new swift expansion in Swedish trade and industry. This provided an opportunity for the Social Democratic government to vastly expand the public sector, to a point where it consumed more than 50 per cent of the gross national product.

Another Social Democratic measure, forced through with the support of the Communists in the autumn of 1983, was to introduce so-called employee funds, aimed at giving the unions greater influence over the economy. This measure had run into fierce and unanimous opposition, both from the non-socialist parties and from employers' organizations, with the result that upon a non-socialist government again coming into power in 1991, the funds were immediately abolished.

Despite losses at the 1985 elections, the socialist parties had retained a majority, so Palme's government remained in power. The chief change at these elections had been the Liberals' unexpected success under their new leader Bengt Westerberg. At the same time the Moderates were still the biggest non-socialist party, a position they would still further strengthen at the 1988 and 1991 elections.

For almost 200 years Swedes had been spared political assassinations, and the murder of Olof Palme by persons unknown, on February 28, 1986, came as an immense shock to the whole nation. He was immediately succeeded as prime minister by Ingvar Carlsson, who in all essentials pursued the same policies. Nor were there any great cabinet changes. Palme's assassination, however, reduced the role of foreign policy in Swedish public debate and led to a concomitant falling off in the Swedish government's involvement in, and influence on, international affairs as compared with the Palme period.

Ever since the 1970s the environmental threats posed by a technological, ever more urbanized society have been an important political issue. And after the 1988 elections, which it

143

dominated, a new party, the Greens, entered Parliament. Even if the Greens failed to win the required 4 per cent of all votes in the 1991 elections, the party made its comeback in 1995 with 5 per cent, and since then its presence in Parliament seems assured. Ever since the mid-1980s the Greens' role has been an important one, both in and outside Parliament, in increasing public interest in environmental questions.

Though the Social Democrats had lost 3 seats at the 1988 elections, they had still had more votes than the three non-socialist parties together; and so remained in power. Nor had

Olof Palme, leader of the Social Democratic Party 1969–86, and prime minister 1969–76 and 1982–86, here seen talking with African National Congress leader Oliver Tambo at an anti-apartheid conference in Stockholm in Feb 1986, just before Palme's assassination. From 1968 onwards, when he sided openly with the Vietnamese liberation movement, his dominant characteristic was a profound commitment to the struggle against apartheid and political oppression everywhere. – Pressens Bild/Peter Berggren.

144

their prospects of implementing their policies dwindled. Together with the Communists they still enjoyed an absolute majority and were thus not dependent upon the politically unstable Greens.

The 1980s saw an end to the rise in production growth that had so far been typical of the Swedish economy, notably during the 1950s and 1960s. As the decade ended, and during the first years of the 1990s, industrial production actually fell; whilst at the same time the vast expansion in the public sector was placing ever heavier demands on the national economy. A further factor, here, is increased life expectancy, with a sharp rise in the numbers of pensioners. With almost a fifth of the population in receipt of pensions, the costs of the income-related supplementary pension (ATP) have become so great that the system is having to be revised. By the end of the 1980s the tax burden had become so heavy that it was directly stifling economic growth and strangling production. This was why, in 1990, the Social Democratic government under Ingvar Carlsson, supported by the Liberals, implemented a tax reform that reduced marginal taxation.

At the same time the international trade cycle plunged downwards. Swedish exports fell sharply. Rising unemployment still further burdened the demands already placed on the state's finances by the huge public sector, by necessitating great outlays on such measures as public works, retraining schemes and the introduction of specially subsidized jobs for young people, in addition to normal unemployment benefits. Output fell. The budget deficit grew, and the balance of trade was ever more deeply in the red. Despite the tax reform, dissatisfaction with the Social Democratic régime grew.

The 1991 elections resulted in a substantial shift to the right. The winners, the Moderates, gained 14 seats, while the Liberals and Centre lost 11 apiece. The Social Democrats lost 18 and the Left Party (formerly Communists) 5. At the same time the political scene was changed by the appearance in Parliament of two new parties: the Christian Democrats, KDS, won 26 seats,

145

and the extreme right-wing New Democracy 25. The Greens failed to reach the 4 per cent mark, and lost their 20 seats. The upshot was a clear majority for the non-socialist parties, with 195 seats against 154 for the two socialist parties.

The resignation of the Ingvar Carlsson government was followed by the formation of a non-socialist coalition under Carl Bildt, the chairman of the Moderates, that included the Liberals, the Centre and the Christian Democrats. The government had no absolute parliamentary majority, though in most matters it could count on New-Democrat support.

Under the slogan 'A Fresh Start for Sweden' Carl Bildt's non-socialist government took a number of measures designed to stimulate private enterprise. Important elements in this policy were reduced employers' dues and more favourable conditions for small firms. At the same time the employee funds were dismantled and a number of state-owned concerns privatized. By greater competition with private firms an effort was made within medicine, nursing and other state and municipal branches to raise efficiency and offer greater freedom of choice.

The international economic crisis that fell on Europe in the years 1990–92, however, led to a fall in Swedish production and to swiftly rising unemployment. At the same time a fixed rate of exchange that overvalued the krona caused exports to stagnate, capital exports to rise and a swift rise in the rate of interest. In September 1992 the economic crisis led to an agreement between the government and the Social Democrats that implied heavy cuts and savings in the public sector. Even this, however, did not prevent capital from flowing ever more swiftly out of the country, leading to rising interest rates and a growth in the national debt. In November of that year the government was therefore forced to abandon the fixed exchange rate and allow the krona to float, with a consequent 18 per cent depreciation. But although this stimulated the export industry, unemployment remained high and the budget deficit continued to rise to unacceptable levels.

Where the constitution is concerned, in 1994 Parliament

146

approved an extension of both the parliamentary and local government terms of office from three to four years. As there was a consensus that three-year terms were too short for both voters and elected officials, the decision did not give rise to any political debate.

The 1994 parliamentary elections were heavily influenced by the economic crisis, rising unemployment and the deteriorated conditions in the social welfare system which had set their stamp on the non-socialist government's period of office. The result was a massive victory for the left wing parties, yielding 161 seats for the Social Democrats – an increase of no fewer than 23 – and 22 for the Left Party (formerly Communist) party, i.e., a gain of 6 seats. Furthermore, the Greens were returned with 18 seats, whilst New Democracy only got 1.2 per cent of votes and were excluded.

Even though he had no absolute majority after the 1994 elections Ingvar Carlsson formed a purely Social Democratic government. At first it sought support from the Left Party, which among other proposals had supported the introduction of a supertax *(värnskatt)* on high incomes, together with increases in several other taxes. But for the extremely restrictive economic policy followed by the Social Democratic government since 1995 it has primarly been the Centre Party It has relied on.

At an extra party congress held in March 1995 Ingvar Carlsson, for personal reasons, resigned both the premiership and his chairmanship of the Social Democratic Party. Whereupon Göran Persson, who had been Carlsson's finance minister, was unanimously elected to succeed him. As prime minister Persson, too, formed a single party Social Democratic government, with cabinet shuffles and new faces in most ministerial posts. His policy speech stressed the crucial importance of further reductions in the budget deficit and the need for still more savings, within the framework of a firm economic policy. He detached himself clearly from the Left Party; the Centre Party continues to constitute the government's prime support. A tangible result of this cooperation and the present influence of

147

the Centre Party is the agreement to begin to decommission the nuclear power plant at Barsebäck before the parliamentary elections in 1998.

All these events have changed the political landscape in Sweden, characterized, ever since the 1920s, by a confrontation between a socialist and a non-socialist block. Today the electorate is divided into three: a left wing block consisting of the Left and Green parties, supported by 20–25 per cent of public opinion; a central block of Social Democrats and Centre, with some 40–45 per cent; and, to the right, a non-socialist block consisting of Moderates, Liberals and Christian Democrats, with some 35 per cent of electoral opinion behind them.

As a result of improvements in the trade cycle, especially for the export industry, and of continued cuts in government expenditure more or less along the same lines as were drawn up in 1992 by the non-socialist government, the budget deficit has been reduced and the national debt ceased to grow. Since 1994 this has meant an improvement in the Swedish economy and a stronger krona as against the dollar and D-Mark.

Yet there has been a price to pay, in the shape of extensive cutbacks in the social welfare system. Rates of sickness and unemployment benefit have been lowered and very big savings made in the social security and medical services. This has unleashed protests and demonstrations against the Social Democratic government. Nor have labour market measures, though attracting a lot of attention, led to any radical fall in unemployment, which today still remains the most serious problem confronting Swedish society.

# Problems and Trends

## Sweden's Origins

There are many ways of looking at Sweden's history, and her development can be depicted in various perspectives. It was the Swedish historian and poet Erik Gustaf Geijer (1783–1847) who originated the saying that 'Sweden's history is the history of her kings'. And for many generations the state's political history was written in accordance with this idea. During the late nineteenth century, however, attention also came to focus on cultural developments. Not until the twentieth century did Sweden's economic history begin to be the object of research and taken as the starting point for describing events and trends. Since World War II social structures and trends have come to be more and more considered in this light and provide such a basis.

The question of Sweden's origins is connected with whether by 'Sweden' one means the country as a kingdom, as a state or as a nation, and how these concepts are to be defined. Our starting point here is to ask: at what level does the individual confront the power of society – i.e., the collective that gives shape to laws and norms and the social organs that enact and ensure obedience to them?

Research, both historical and archeological, shows that during the Viking Age or the early Middle Ages no Swedish kingdom or realm, in our modern sense of the word, as yet existed. The individual was concerned with a society that operated at clan or tribal level and in small local units. Even if some prominent Viking chieftain could at times subsume groups of petty kings

150

under his sway, in loosely knit and unstable realms, this had little or no bearing on the life or activities of the individual. These were enacted within the framework of local communities and rural areas.

Christianity, introduced in the twelfth century, divided Sweden up into parishes and dioceses. And at the same time legislation and its enforcement became the task of the 'hundred' and county. Not until the thirteenth century, with Birger Jarl and Magnus Ladulås, can we speak of a firmly established Swedish kingdom.

## The Power of the State

During the High Middle Ages and the Union Period, from the mid-thirteenth century to the beginning of the sixteenth, the unit within which the law was enforced, taxes were paid and administration organized was the castle fief. Swedish history during the Union Period was fraught with struggles for power over these fiefs which, with the passage of time, clustered into ever larger units.

Partly thanks to the execution of most of his competitors in the Stockholm Bloodbath of 1520, Gustav Vasa managed to gather in his own hands total power over the country's fiefs. During the 1540s he organized, along German lines, a central administration in the shape of an exchequer and a chancery under his own immediate supervision. It was this that made Sweden into a state, with norms established and centrally administered by the king and his bureaucracy.

After the death of Gustav Vasa in 1560, the Vasa Period (1523–1654) was fraught with struggles between the king and the nobility for power over the state's administration. The 1634 Constitution organized the administration in its central branches directly under the Council. However, it was not until Karl XI's 'Reduction' and the introduction of absolute monarchy in 1680 that this power struggle was finally resolved. And it was then that the individual found himself confronting the power of

151

society at state level, in the shape of the monarch, his central bureaucracy and local governors.

## The Enlightenment

The Enlightenment was the most important watershed in the history of knowledge and human culture. During the Middle Ages and afterwards up to the eighteenth century, yesterday was always regarded as having been happier than tomorrow could be – one spoke of 'the good old days'.

It was in the eighteenth century, inspired by such thinkers as Descartes in France and Locke in Britain, that people began to rely on their own thinking and ability to discover the laws of nature and reason. They abandoned the religious doctrines that had hitherto constrained free thought. They discovered nature, realized it was subject to its own laws, and explored it greedily and experimentally. At the same time they began to look critically at society and its structures, analyse its functions and reform its organization. The basis for the whole of this development was a belief in man's own faculties and the power of free thought. And the conclusion? That developments always went forward, that the world would be better and happier tomorrow than it is today or was yesterday.

Optimism about the future and the doctrine of progress has played a crucial role in western culture and secured its spread over the earth in the nineteenth and twentieth centuries. It has been the condition for forceful analysis of nature as well as of problems provided by society and the individual.

At international level Isaac Newton and his disciples were the first to research nature's laws and apply them in the service of humanity. On a theoretical level such attitudes were explored by Voltaire and Rousseau, by Montesquieu and Diderot in their Encyclopaedia. On the level of practical politics this led to the demand for liberty, equality and fraternity that unleashed the French Revolution.

152

Such ideas had swiftly established themselves in eighteenth-century Sweden. Such geniuses as Christopher Polhem and Emanuel Swedenborg, Linnaeus and Anders Celsius explored the laws of nature and technology. The constitution of the Age of Freedom evidences the growth, also in Sweden, of demands for constitutional government and representative influence. After temporary reverses during the reigns of Gustav III and Gustav IV Adolf developments led to the 1809 Constitution, which provided the basis for development in the direction of a constitutional monarchy and a democratic society.

During the nineteenth century the idea that all power stems from the people became a generally accepted element in public debate. The authoritarian state was criticized. The earlier part of the century gave rise to demands for liberal reforms. And by the mid-century this resulted in a number of such reforms, freeing the individual from bondage to the state and increasing his influence, both locally and at state level. The restrictive guild system was abolished in 1846, communal legislation introduced in 1862 and a fully representative parliament in 1866.

## National Romanticism and Industrial Breakthrough

In the humanistic sciences of the nineteenth century people began to concern themselves with their own origins and history. In art and literature a national romanticism flourished, inspired by Herder's philosophy and Goethe's poetry in Germany, Macpherson's *The Songs of Ossian* in Scotland, and Walter Scott's novels in England. In Sweden these trends found expression in the founding of the Geatish Association in 1811 and, in poetry, in for instance Geijer's 'The Viking' and 'The Yeoman Farmer', and Esaias Tegnér's *Frithiof's Saga*.

As late as during the French Revolution and the First Empire anyone who adopted the revolution's fundamental ideas of liberty, equality and fraternity was regarded in Europe as a fully fledged citizen. It was in the struggle to liberate the countries from the grip of Napoleon, however, that nationalism was born. And it was national romanticism that fertilized the notion that the links that held together what now came to be called 'the nation state' were common language and culture – not the hereditary rights of some princely family, usually derived from victory in warfare. On the continent of Europe this led to a united Germany and a united Italy.

The industrial breakthrough lent extra weight to demands for national autonomy. In nineteenth-century and early twentieth-century Europe industry developed within national frameworks, each state deciding over its own economy's norms and conditions. The development and growing strength of the nation states, together with their rivalries, led to the European catastrophe of World War I.

In Sweden, where industrialization did not begin until during the later part of the nineteenth century, national feeling grew at the same pace as public education. During the first half of the century it took the form of among other things pan-Scandinavianism, but, after this movement had misfired in the 1860s, turned into a Swedish patriotism heavily backed up by conservative elements in the upper and middle classes.

Around the mid-century, however, nationalism found a broader basis in liberal interest in public education and the introduction of universal elementary schools. Such popular movements as teetotalism, the non-denominational churches and the workers' movement lent fresh impetus to Swedish national self-awareness. Yet it was not until the first decades of the twentieth century, after the Social Democratic movement had abandoned its revolutionary ideology and the labour movement, under the impact of World War I, had become more and more self-consciously Swedish, that the nation as a whole became unambiguously aware of itself.

It is from that moment we can date Sweden's birth as a nation. At the same time parliamentary government was celebrating its definitive breakthrough; the universal franchise was introduced,

154

and Sweden became a democratically governed state. Further strength to Swedish nationalism has since then been derived from such factors as general support for welfare policies at home and neutrality abroad.

The 1870–1970 period has been called 'the Swedish economy's hundred brilliant years' – a long period, typified by virtually uninterrupted economic progress. Characteristic of Sweden was not merely the swiftness of its growth but above all its uniquely unbroken continuity.

It was in the 1870s that the timber industry had made its great breakthrough. Simultaneously, the introduction of new methods into the steel industry led to an expansion in the metals industry as a whole. During the century's last two decades new, so-called genius industries flourished on the basis of such notable Swedish inventions as Alfred Nobel's dynamite, Lars Magnus Ericsson's automatic telephone, Gustaf de Laval's cream separator, Nils Gustav Dalén's acetylene gas lighting and automatic lighthouses, Jonas Wenström's electric generators and motors and – somewhat later – Sven Wingquist's self-regulating ball bearing. All these gave rise to companies which still today constitute the basis upon which the Swedish welfare state rests.

## The Welfare State

Up to World War I the swift developments in Swedish industry were largely financed by foreign capital. Sweden was a net borrower. But as a consequence of her neutrality, her considerable war profits and the evaporation of her foreign debts after Germany's defeat in 1918, her economic situation underwent an abrupt change. During the 1920s the major Swedish concerns set up subsidiaries abroad. This made her a net lender, with the greatest number of multinational concerns, in proportion to the population, of any country in the world.

Thanks to a cautious, at times opportunistic policy of neutrality, Sweden managed to avoid being dragged into World War II.

When it was over came the so-called harvest time. Welfare and security were guaranteed the individual by general child allowances, sickness insurance, rising old age pensions, a national supplementary pension, an extensive house-building programme and by extensions both of schools and higher education. At the same time this entailed higher taxes and the creation of a huge public sector. The social welfare state thus created – the so-called Swedish model – became an object of study and, to a varying extent, emulation all over the world.

But its basis lay in the swift growth of the country's industry and economy. During the 1950s and 1960s full employment, swiftly growing output and a positive balance of trade made possible the reforms then carried through.

## Sweden and the European Union

In post-World War II Europe it was generally understood that the national frameworks within which economies and industries had hitherto developed no longer met the need for economic collaboration, free movement across frontiers and international competition. The upshot was the creation, in 1957, of the European Community (EC), originally comprising six countries only, but which in 1972 was expanded to include two more and, during the 1970s, a total of twelve.

The end of the Cold War in 1989 changed Sweden's international position. Neutrality, which up to then had prevented her joining EC, no longer had the same role to play. And this brought to a head the question of whether Sweden should or should not join the Community. In Sweden, as elsewhere in Europe, it was seen as obvious that the nation state was in many spheres too narrow a framework for laws and regulations, in terms of their legislation, their application and their enforcement. Strong demands were made, e.g. in the Swedish Social Democratic Party, for the creation of political organs on the same level as the multinational companies. This led in 1991 to a Swedish application for membership of the European Community, a victory for the Yes line in the 1994 referendum, and to EU membership in 1995.

This is not to say that Sweden's continued membership has not been much debated, in particular the third phase of the Economic and Monetary Union (EMU), i.e., the introduction of a common currency and a central bank. In reality it also bears on future collaboration within EU.

In the last instance the problem turns upon the fact that the need for supranational and uniform rules is not identical in all fields. There is no question of the need for a wider economic and industrial framework, i.e. that the individual or commercial concern shall confront social authority at a level superior to that of the nation state. The same applies to environmental questions and crime abatement. But when it comes to social and welfare policy the situation is different. In this field there is no great need for international uniformity. On the contrary. Each country – notably Sweden – is concerned to preserve its own welfare system as it has grown up within its frameworks and is anchored in national, social and cultural developments. The same applies to such countries as Denmark and the Netherlands and to Belgium and the catholic countries of southern Europe, where religious norms set their stamp on the shape of social policy.

Thus the great dilemma for Sweden in the EU question is that the need for supranational and uniform norms is not the same in all spheres. No one questions its relevance to the economy, industry, environmental policy or crime abatement. But it does not apply to social policy, nor to the financial policies that hang thereon. Thus Sweden's attitude to EU is determined by which of these questions shall be given priority. In today's Sweden the preservation of the Swedish model, with its large public sector and an extensive and smoothly functioning system of social security, is high on the list of desiderata. In the last instance the question here – as so often before in Swedish history – is: at what level shall the individual confront society, its powers and organization?

(All datings up to the end of the twelfth century are unsure and only approximative.)

| | | | |
|---|---|---|---|
| Olof Skötkonung | 990s–1022 | Sten Sture the Elder | 1501–1503 |
| Anund Jakob | 1022–1050 | Svante Nilsson Sture | 1504–1511 |
| Emund the Old | 1050–1060 | Sten Sture the Younger | 1512–1520 |
| Stenkil | 1060–1066 | Kristian II | 1520–1521 |
| Halsten | 1066–1080s | | |
| Inge the Elder | 1080s–1110s | The Vasa Dynasty | |
| Inge the Younger | 1118–1120s | Gustav Vasa | 1521 (1523)–1560 |
| | | Erik XIV | 1560–1568 |
| The Sverker and Erik Clans | | Johan III | 1568–1592 |
| Sverker the Elder | 1135–1156 | Sigismund | 1592–1599 |
| Saint Erik | 1156–1160 | Karl IX | (1592–) 1599 (1604)–1611 |
| Karl Sverkersson | 1160–1167 | Gustav II Adolf | 1611–1632 |
| Knut Eriksson | 1167–1195 (1196) | Kristina's regency | 1632–1644 |
| Sverker the Younger Karlsson | 1196–1208 | Kristina | (1632) 1644–1654 |
| Erik Knutsson | 1208–1216 | | |
| Johan Sverkersson | 1216–1222 | The Palatinate Dynasty | |
| Erik Eriksson (a minor) | 1222–1229 | Karl X Gustav | 1654–1660 |
| Knut Holmgersson (The Tall) | 1229–1234 | Karl XI's regency | 1660–1672 |
| Erik Eriksson (The Lisping and Lame) | 1234–1249 | Karl XI | (1660) 1672–1697 |
| | | Karl XII's regency | 1697 |
| The Folkunga Dynasty | | Karl XII | 1697–1718 |
| Birger Jarl, guardian and *jarl* | 1250–1266 | Ulrika Eleonora | 1719–1720 |
| Valdemar Birgersson | (1250) 1266–1275 | | |
| Magnus Birgersson (Ladulås) | 1275–1290 | The Hessian Dynasty | |
| Birger Magnusson's regency | 1290–1298 | Fredrik I | 1720–1751 |
| Birger Magnusson | (1290) 1298–1318 | | |
| Magnus Eriksson's regency | 1319–c.1332 | The Holstein–Gottorp Dynasty | |
| Magnus Eriksson | (1319) c.1332–1364 | Adolf Fredrik | 1751–1771 |
| | | Gustav III | 1771–1792 |
| The Mecklenburg Dynasty | | Gustav IV Adolf's regency | 1792–1796 |
| Albrekt of Mecklenburg | (1363) 1364–1389 | Gustav IV Adolf | (1792) 1796–1809 |
| | | Karl XIII | 1809–1818 |
| Union Regents and Lords Protector | | | |
| Margareta | 1389–1412 | The Bernadotte Dynasty | |
| Erik of Pomerania (1397) | 1412–1434 (1439) | Karl XIV Johan | 1818–1844 |
| Kristoffer of Bavaria | 1441–1448 | Oskar I | 1844–1859 |
| Karl Knutsson | 1448–1457 | Karl XV | 1859–1872 |
| Kristian I | 1457–1464 | Oskar II | 1872–1907 |
| Karl Knutsson | 1464–1465, 1467–1470 | Gustaf V | 1907–1950 |
| Sten Sture the Elder | 1471–1497 | Gustaf VI Adolf | 1950–1973 |
| Hans | 1497–1501 | Carl XVI Gustaf | 1973– |

# SWEDEN'S WARS AND PEACE TREATIES AFTER THE DISSOLUTION OF THE KALMAR UNION IN 1523

| | |
|---|---|
| 1534-36 | Sweden joins in the Count's Feud, in which Kristian II is hindered from regaining the Danish crown with Lübeck's support. |
| 1563-70 | The Nordic Seven Years War against Denmark. Peace of Stettin, 1570: the Älvsborg ransom. |
| 1570-83 | War with Russia for control of Estonia. |
| 1590-95 | War with Russia. Peace of Teusina, 1595: Narva and Estonia become Swedish. |
| 1611-13 | The 'Kalmar War' against Denmark. Peace of Knäred, 1613: second Älvsborg ransom. |
| 1617 | Peace of Stolbova: Russia renounces Keksholm province and Ingermanland. |
| 1621-29 | War with Poland for Livonia 1621-26, and for the Prussian harbours 1626-29. Armistice of Altmark, 1629: Livonia and several Prussian harbours become Swedish for six years. |
| 1630-48 | Sweden participates in the Thirty Years War. The Heilbronn League, 1633. |
| 1643-45 | War with Denmark. Lennart Torstenson invades Holstein in 1643. Peace of Brömsebro, 1645: Sweden obtains Jämtland, Härjedalen, Gotland, Ösel, Halland for thirty years, as well as exemption of tolls in Öresund. |
| 1640 | Peace of Westphalia signed at Osnabrück and Münster: Sweden obtains part of Pomerania with Rügen, Stettin, Wismar, Usedom and Wollin as well as the duchies of Bremen and Verden. |
| 1655-60 | War with Poland: Karl X Gustav seizes Cracow 1655. Denmark declares war 1657. |
| 1656-61 | War with Russia. Peace of Kardis: no territorial concessions. |
| 1657-58 | War with Denmark. Peace of Roskilde, 1658: Sweden obtains Skåne, Blekinge, Halland, Bohuslän, Trondheim province and Bornholm. |
| 1658-60 | War with Denmark. |
| 1660 | Peace of Oliwa with Poland: Livonia becomes Swedish. Peace of Copenhagen with Denmark, which recovers Trondheim province and Bornholm. |
| 1674-75 | Brandenburg War. Sweden defeated at Fehrbellin 1675. Denmark declares war. |

| | |
|---|---|
| 1675-79 | War with Denmark—the 'Skåne War'. Treaty of Lund, 1679: no territorial concessions. |
| 1679 | France and Sweden make peace with Brandenburg at Fontainebleau and Sweden has to give up part of Pomerania. |
| 1700-21 | The Great Northern War. |
| 1719 | Peace of Stockholm with Hanover: Bremen and Verden given up. |
| 1720 | Peace with Prussia: Western Pomerania as far as the Peene River and Usedom and Wollin given up. Peace of Fredriksborg with Denmark: Sweden agrees to pay tolls in Öresund again. |
| 1721 | Peace of Nystad with Russia: Livonia, Estonia, Ingermanland and part of Karelia given up. |
| 1741-43 | War with Russia, the 'Hats' War'. Peace of Åbo, 1743: territory east of Kymmene River given up. |
| 1757-63 | Pomeranian War, the Seven Years War. Peace of Hamburg: no territorial concessions. |
| 1788-90 | Gustav III's Russian war. Peace with Denmark, 1789. Peace of Värälä with Russia, 1790. No territorial concessions. |
| 1805-07 | War in Pomerania. Sweden joins Britain, Hanover and Russia against Napoleon. French troops attack Swedish Pomerania 1807. Treaty of Tilsit between France and Russia. |
| 1808-09 | War in Finland. Russia attacks in February, Denmark in March. Peace of Fredrikshamn: all Finland, including the Åland islands, given up. Peace of Jönköping with Denmark: no territorial concessions. |
| 1810 | Treaty of Paris with France. Sweden regains Pomerania but is forced to join the Continental System and declare war on Britain. |
| 1812 | Napoleon occupies Swedish Pomerania. Sweden signs treaty with Russia. |
| 1813 | Sweden joins in attack on Napoleon in Germany. Karl Johan attacks Napoleon's ally Denmark. |
| 1814 | Treaty of Kiel. The Swedish king elected king of Norway and Norway forced into union with Sweden. Swedish Pomerania to Denmark in exchange. |
| 1814 | War with Norway ends with Convention of Moss, August 14, 1814. |

159

# PRIME MINISTERS AND PARTIES IN POWER FROM 1876

| | | | | |
|---|---|---|---|---|
| Louis De Geer | 1876–1880 | Per Albin Hansson, | | |
| Arvid Posse | 1880–1883 | National coalition | 1939–1945 | |
| Carl Johan Thyselius | 1883–1884 | Per Albin Hansson, | | |
| Oscar Robert Themptander | 1884–1888 | Social Democrat | 1945–1946 | |
| Gillis Bildt | 1888–1889 | Tage Erlander, | | |
| Gustaf Åkerhielm | 1889–1891 | Social Democrat | 1946–1951 | |
| Erik Gustaf Boström | 1891–1900 | Tage Erlander, | | |
| Fredrik von Otter | 1900–1902 | Social-Democratic- | | |
| Erik Gustaf Boström | 1902–1905 | Agrarian coalition | 1951–1957 | |
| Johan Ramstedt | 1905 | Tage Erlander, | | |
| Christian Lundeberg | 1905 | Social Democrat | 1957–1969 | |
| Karl Staaff, Liberal | 1905–1906 | Olof Palme, | | |
| Arvid Lindman, Conservative | 1906–1911 | Social Democrat | 1969–1976 | |
| Karl Staaff, Liberal | 1911–1914 | Thorbjörn Fälldin, | | |
| Hjalmar Hammarskjöld, | | Centre-Moderate- | | |
| Civil servant ministry | 1914–1917 | Liberal coalition | 1976–1978 | |
| Carl Swartz, Conservative | 1917 | Ola Ullsten, Liberal | 1978–1979 | |
| Nils Edén, Liberal-Social- | | Thorbjörn Fälldin, | | |
| Democratic coalition | 1917–1920 | Centre-Moderate- | | |
| Hjalmar Branting, | | Liberal coalition | 1979–1981 | |
| Social Democrat | 1920 | Thorbjörn Fälldin, | | |
| Louis De Geer, Non-party | 1920–1921 | Centre-Liberal coalition | 1981–1982 | |
| Oscar von Sydow, Non-party | 1921 | Olof Palme, | | |
| Hjalmar Branting, | | Social Democrat | 1982–1986 | |
| Social Democrat | 1921–1923 | Ingvar Carlsson, | | |
| Ernst Trygger, Conservative | 1923–1924 | Social Democrat | 1986–1991 | |
| Hjalmar Branting, | | Carl Bildt, Moderate-Liberal- | | |
| Social Democrat | 1924–1925 | Centre-Christian | | |
| Rickard Sandler, | | Democratic coalition | 1991–1994 | |
| Social Democrat | 1925–1926 | Ingvar Carlsson, | | |
| Carl Gustaf Ekman, Liberal | 1926–1928 | Social Democrat | 1994–1996 | |
| Arvid Lindman, Conservative | 1928–1930 | Göran Persson, | | |
| Carl Gustaf Ekman, Liberal | 1930–1932 | Social Democrat | 1996– | |
| Felix Hamrin, Liberal | 1932 | | | |
| Per Albin Hansson, | | | | |
| Social Democrat | 1932–1936 | | | |
| Axel Pehrsson-Bramstorp, | | | | |
| Agrarian | 1936 | | | |
| Per Albin Hansson, | | | | |
| Social-Democratic- | | | | |
| Agrarian coalition | 1936–1939 | | | |

Names of parties are given from the 1905 Staaff government onwards, since it was only from that moment that political parties, in the modern sense of the word, began to exert a decisive influence on the composition of cabinets.

**POLITICAL PARTIES** (seats in Parliament)

| | FIRST CHAMBER | | | | | | SECOND CHAMBER | | | | | |
|---|---|---|---|---|---|---|---|---|---|---|---|---|
| Year | Conservative, from 1969 Moderate Party | Agrarian, from 1958 Centre Party | Liberals | Social Democrats | Communists | Total | Conservative, from 1969 Moderate Party | Agrarian, from 1958 Centre Party | Liberals | Social Democrats | Communists | Total |
| 1912 | 86 | – | 52 | 12 | – | 150 | 64 | – | 102 | 64 | – | 230 |
| 1914 | 88 | – | 49 | 13 | – | 150 | 36 | – | 70 | 74 | – | 230 |
| 1915 | 89 | – | 47 | 14 | – | 150 | 36 | – | 57 | 87 | – | 230 |
| 1918 | 88 | – | 45 | 17 | – | 150 | 57 | 14 | 62 | 97 | – | 230 |
| 1921 | 37 | 19 | 40 | 51 | 3 | 150 | 71 | 30 | 47 | 80 | 2 | 230 |
| 1922 | 41 | 18 | 38 | 52 | 1 | 150 | 62 | 21 | 41 | 99 | 7 | 230 |
| 1925 | 44 | 18 | 35 | 52 | 1 | 150 | 65 | 23 | 33 | 104 | 5 | 230 |
| 1929 | 49 | 17 | 31 | 52 | 1 | 150 | 73 | 27 | 32 | 90 | 8 | 230 |
| 1933 | 50 | 18 | 23 | 53 | 1 | 150 | 58 | 36 | 24 | 104 | 8 | 230 |
| 1937 | 45 | 22 | 16 | 66 | 1 | 150 | 44 | 36 | 27 | 112 | 11 | 230 |
| 1941 | 35 | 24 | 15 | 75 | 1 | 150 | 42 | 28 | 23 | 134 | 3 | 230 |
| 1945 | 30 | 21 | 14 | 83 | 2 | 150 | 39 | 35 | 26 | 115 | 15 | 230 |
| 1949 | 24 | 21 | 18 | 84 | 3 | 150 | 23 | 30 | 57 | 112 | 8 | 230 |
| 1953 | 20 | 25 | 22 | 79 | 4 | 150 | 31 | 26 | 58 | 110 | 5 | 230 |
| 1957 | 13 | 25 | 30 | 79 | 3 | 150 | 42 | 19 | 58 | 106 | 6 | 231 |
| 1958 | 16 | 24 | 29 | 79 | 3 | 151 | 45 | 32 | 38 | 111 | 5 | 231 |
| 1961 | 19 | 20 | 33 | 77 | 2 | 151 | 39 | 34 | 40 | 114 | 5 | 232 |
| 1965 | 26 | 19 | 26 | 73 | 2 | 151 | 33 | 36 | 43 | 113 | 8 | 233 |
| 1969 | 25 | 20 | 26 | 79 | 1 | 151 | 32 | 39 | 34 | 125 | 3 | 233 |

## SINGLE-CHAMBER PARLIAMENT (distribution of seats and percentually)

| Year | Moderate Party | % | Centre Party | % | Liberals | % | Social Democrats | % | Communists from 1990 Left Party | % | Green Party | % | Christian Democrats | % | New democracy | % | Total |
|---|---|---|---|---|---|---|---|---|---|---|---|---|---|---|---|---|---|
| 1970 | 41 | 11.5 | 71 | 19.9 | 58 | 16.2 | 163 | 45.3 | 17 | 4.8 | | | | | | | 350 |
| 1973 | 51 | 14.3 | 90 | 25.1 | 34 | 9.4 | 156 | 43.6 | 19 | 5.3 | | | | | | | 350 |
| 1976 | 55 | 15.6 | 86 | 24.1 | 39 | 11.1 | 152 | 42.7 | 17 | 4.8 | | | | | | | 349 |
| 1979 | 73 | 20.3 | 64 | 18.1 | 38 | 10.6 | 154 | 43.2 | 20 | 5.6 | | | | | | | 349 |
| 1982 | 86 | 23.6 | 56 | 15.5 | 21 | 5.9 | 166 | 45.6 | 20 | 5.6 | — | | | | | | 349 |
| 1985 | 76 | 21.3 | 44 | 12.4* | 51 | 14.2 | 159 | 44.7 | 19 | 5.4 | — | | | | | | 349 |
| 1988 | 66 | 18.3 | 42 | 11.3 | 44 | 12.2 | 156 | 43.2 | 21 | 5.8 | 20 | 5.5 | | | | | 349 |
| 1991 | 80 | 21.9 | 31 | 8.5 | 33 | 9.1 | 138 | 37.7 | 16 | 4.5 | 0 | 3.4 | 26 | 7.1 | 25 | 6.7 | 349 |
| 1994 | 80 | 22.4 | 27 | 7.7 | 26 | 7.2 | 161 | 45.3 | 22 | 6.2 | 18 | 5.0 | 15 | 4.1 | 0 | 1.2 | 349 |

Independent members and also minor parties have been added to the major party they stood closest to. *Together with the Christian Democratic Party (KDS)

# SVENSKA
## I N S T I T U T E T

The SWEDISH INSTITUTE is a government-financed foundation established to disseminate knowledge abroad about Sweden's social and cultural life, to promote cultural and informational exchange with other countries and to contribute to increased international cooperation in the fields of education and research. The Swedish Institute produces a wide range of publications on many aspects of Swedish society. These publications can be obtained from Swedish missions abroad or directly from the Swedish Institute.

In the SWEDEN BOOKSHOP you will find – in several foreign languages – books, brochures, fact sheets and richly illustrated gift books on Sweden, a broad selection of Swedish fiction and children's books as well as music, slides, video cassettes and Swedish language courses.

*Visit*
the SWEDEN BOOKSHOP, Sweden House
at Hamngatan/Kungsträdgården in Stockholm

*Read*
the home page of the Swedish Institute: http://www.si.se

*Phone*
Customer Service: + 46-8-789 20 00

*Write to*
SVENSKA INSTITUTET
Box 7434, S–103 91 Stockholm, Sweden
Fax + 46-8-20 72 48 • E-mail: order@si.se